The Author, George King, D.D.

COVER PHOTOGRAPH. The author explains the technique of Spiritual Healing, as described in this book, which he has demonstrated many times in the past to public audiences in England and America.

This book is printed and published by The Aetherius Society, a Religious, Educational and Charitable Organization.

YOU TOO CAN
HEAL

By George King, D.D.

Printed and Published by
THE AETHERIUS SOCIETY
6202 Afton Place, Los Angeles, California 90028, U.S.A.

DELUXE EDITION

First Published — April 1976
Second Impression — February 1990

YOU TOO CAN HEAL

COPYRIGHT OWNED BY
GEORGE KING, D.D.

YOU TOO CAN HEAL is printed and published by The Aetherius Society, 6202 Afton Place, Hollywood, California 90028-8298, U.S.A.

Manufactured in the United States of America.

CONTENTS

ILLUSTRATIONS

DEDICATION

This book is dedicated to those Spiritual Healers everywhere who, without thought of personal reward, have helped to relieve the suffering of mankind.

INTRODUCTION

Here, at last, is the textbook on Spiritual Healing that you have always needed. You have this book in your hand because you are interested in Healing; perhaps only mildly, or perhaps you are very interested. If you are only mildly interested, it may be because you have not had access to the information and exposure to Spiritual Healing that you should have had. This book will unveil the mystery which surrounds this subject and bring Spiritual Healing right out into the open for what it is: one of the most powerful and effective means possible for you, or anyone else, to demonstrate your compassion for the suffering of your fellow men.

If you are very interested, then the chances are that you, too, need information because, let us face it, there has not been much information available up to this time.

"You Too Can Heal" will change all of that!

This book will tell the aspiring healer why he should begin now and no longer hesitate. It will give him the inspiration and the confidence which he has probably always needed. It will show him that Spiritual Healing, like everything else worth doing, is very largely a matter of having the right knowledge and then applying that knowledge under correct guidance. This book provides all of that.

The healer who is just beginning has already gained some experience. His belief and Faith have been enough to get him started. What he needs now is the experience and guidance of an expert. He wants desperately to know exactly what Spiritual Healing is, how it works and why it works. He also needs a solid technique to smooth out the rough spots and to tell him what to do in the numerous different situations which he will meet while giving Healing.

The practising healer needs all of these things and more. He has already met with success and failure. His successes will have strengthened his Faith in the Power of God, but his failures should have increased his dissatisfaction with his performance as a healer. Perhaps more than anyone, he needs—and he knows he needs—the expert guidance which this book provides.

The author of this book accepts Healing as one of the great, natural processes of life—and so should you. After all, you have given Healing, or received it, practically every day of your life! It is not possible for two persons to pass on the street, let alone for them to shake hands or strike up a conversation, without some interchange of subtle magnetic forces taking place. One is bound to be stronger, more optimistic, in better general health than the other. An exchange takes place and the weaker of the two benefits. Such Healing takes place between all living things at all times. It is instinctive and unconscious. What makes a person a really good healer is when the interchange of natural forces is done consciously and deliberately. To show you how to do this is the purpose of this book.

Doctor George King, who wrote this book for you, is eminently qualified to teach Spiritual Healing. He is one of the truly great Spiritual healers of the world who, from fairly ordinary beginnings as a healer has gone on to carry Healing to extraordinary heights. Today he heads an international Spiritual Order, The Aetherius Society, which is dedicated to world Peace and Enlightenment through selfless Service to humanity. Doctor King is a Master of Yoga, regarded in knowing circles as one of the world's leading Occultists, with an extremely rare specialization in the manipulation of Spiritual energies! When he talks about Spiritual Healing, he talks about the use of those very energies of the Cosmos which are available to us all in infinite abundance; energies which he can see and direct and the characteristics of which he knows more about and can do more with, than almost any other person alive today! Because he *knows* these energies so well. Because he *knows* that they are available to us all, quite literally at our finger tips, he is saddened by how little use we make of the infinite, magnificent reservoir of Divine Power! In this book, he shows us how to use these mighty forces to heal through the restoration of the natural balance of these energies within the complex human structure.

This is emphatically not a book on Faith Healing, or of Healing through diet or herbal remedies. Those forms of Healing have their adherents and they have provided millions with relief from pain and suffering all over the world. There are numerous books on these subjects and you can learn much of great value from the best of them.

"You Too Can Heal" concerns itself with the most powerful, most direct, most natural form of Spiritual Healing the world has ever known. *To the best of my knowledge it is the first book of its kind ever published!*

A word of caution before you begin your practise of Spiritual Healing. Your city, state, county or country may have regulations affecting Spiritual Healing. You should find out about these regulations to avoid being prosecuted under civil law for performing your Spiritual duty.

Now go on and read the well-explained text written by a healer who truly knows. Follow the simple directions and study the clear illustrations. Use this as a textbook.

Do not be afraid of it!

Before you realize what has happened, the great balancing forces of Life, itself, will flow through you into another, ridding them of conditions which have caused them endless suffering and which may even have defied the medical profession. Then you will know that YOU TOO CAN HEAL!

Reverend Charles E. Abrahamson.

PLATE 1, overleaf, shows a mass Healing meeting in the famous cultural centre, the Caxton Hall in London, held by the author on September 2nd, 1972 at the end of his successful lecture tour of Britain. To comply with the fire regulations, the doors to this meeting had to be closed before it started as there was only standing room left. Doctor King put a dozen trained healers on the platform and free Spiritual Healing treatments were given to over 50 members of the audience who desired them. Many people who received Contact Healing at this meeting in London commented on the success of the treatment afterwards. All the Spiritual healers on the platform were using the technique described in this book.

INTRODUCTION TO THE AUTHOR

George King was born on January 23rd, 1919, in Wellington, Shropshire, England. From the beginning a profoundly Religious child, he became closely attached to orthodox Christianity. In particular the Christian compassion for suffering and the works of many devout Christians to relieve suffering, struck a chord deep in his very being. Although not many years passed before the limitations of orthodoxy became apparent to him, his early attraction to the relief of suffering in all forms never deserted him. On the contrary, as you will shortly see, it took on deeper and more powerful forms as the years passed. In these earlier years, however, he found himself strongly drawn to the fact that man could, even through simple but strongly felt Prayer, cure some of the sickness and disease he saw in those around him.

Then came World War II. George King was non-violent by personal conviction and, instead of serving with the armed forces of Great Britain, he served with distinction in the National Fire Service in the years of unbelievable danger and destruction of the Battle of Britain. During this time, some of the major cities of England were in flames from the Nazi bombings and the dread V-1's and V-2's which came later. It is significant that during the long years of this terrible conflict, George King gave recognition to his responsibilities to mankind by helping to protect and save life and in the relief of human suffering.

When the war was over, George King was able to resume his own personal interests and undertook a serious study of psychic phenomena. Throwing all of his energies into this research—an outlook which would typify the intensity of purpose which, to this very day, stamps his every action—he very quickly began to perceive the causes underlying surface effects. The book of mysteries began to open its pages to him. It was not long before he could recognize the causes of most of the evils which beset this world. Sickness, ignorance, ruthless power, none of these were accidental or coincidental. Their effects were caused. To the young man, George King, it was obvious that life had a major purpose; to isolate the causes and find the cure!

More ordinary men would have studied economics, medicine, or even gone into law, politics or the Church. George King delved and progressed deeper into paranormal phenomena where the real relation of cause to effect is hidden. In this enchanted land of psychic sights and sounds, many researchers are trapped, their awareness of the basic world of men becoming increasingly warped or lost altogether. But to George King it became a laboratory for vital experimentation which led him to discover the precise laws and formulae which operate on these planes of existence. His knowledge, discrimination and detachment grew until it became virtually impossible for him to be deceived or misled in the field of psychic phenomena.

His exhaustive preparations behind him, George King began demonstrating his acutely developed psychic abilities. It was only a matter of time before he had successfully and repeatedly demonstrated the psychic powers then commonly known. Ranking high among these were his powers of Spiritual Healing which led to the performance of virtual "miracles" brought about through his control of the subtle energies which permeate all existence.

Still dissatisfied, and convinced that even greater Truth lay hidden in the richly complicated field of applied Metaphysics, George King began to search for other methods of learning even more about cause, effect and cure. He began to practise Yoga. In those days you did not find schools of Yoga, together with health food shops, academies of the martial arts or short courses on transcendental meditation crowding the major cities of the West as we do today. Such things were not yet popular. If you were interested in them, you had to search for them and often had to prove yourself ready for such information.

Readers of this book should be made aware that, had it not been for the later influence of George King, the current popularity and easy availability of information on subjects of psychical, occult or Metaphysical importance would have been considerably delayed. As one of the prime movers in bringing the Truth to mankind in this century, he saw the scarcity of this kind of information as another kind of suffering which had to be relieved. His later writings, teachings and overall guidance behind the scenes, have had an immense influence on shaping the present day interest in Yoga, Healing, Metaphysics and the Spiritual Sciences.

But let us return to the early days when George King began to study Yoga. Here again, his intensity and determination yielded amazing positive results as he plunged deep into the secrets of this true science. New abilities and increased awareness came until he arrived at a stage where, having mastered terrestrial phenomena, *he rose above it!* No longer was it possible for him to become obsessed or used in ignorance by *any* force or intelligence inhabiting any plane of existence upon Earth. A great battle had been won!

Those were not easy years. Lest anyone think that here was an exceptionally gifted man to whom all came easily without effort, let us set the record straight. George King worked during those years in employment which demanded much of him and he gave that employment his very best. He did not withdraw from the world but worked in it, becoming a true professional in several fields not associated with his major interests! In the meantime, he practised Yoga in his "spare time" for up to 12 hours per day! In other words, the time that the average man spends in play or asleep, George King spent in breathing exercises, contemplation and meditation!

By 1954, George King was practising advanced techniques of Spiritual Healing with the assistance of Intelligences on the higher mental planes with whom he was in contact. These Intelligences, among whom can be listed such great men of medicine and science as Sir James Young Simpson and Sir Oliver Lodge, assisted him in research into more and more effective methods of relieving pain and disease. It was the brilliant Lodge, eminent English physicist who had died in 1940, with whom George King was working on instrumentation for the relief of certain forms of cancer. But Higher Forces had chosen him for an even more important task than this.

George King's ability to project his consciousness led him through a series of advanced Initiations. Thinking of nothing but his self-appointed task of relieving some portion of the burden of man's suffering, he had prepared himself for another important step forward. This step, when it came in May of 1954, took George King far afield from the administration of Spiritual Healing to individuals, although he never forgot nor abandoned his interest in this area.

Let us examine more closely the position in which George King found himself on that May evening in 1954 when his entire world was changed for him by a unique mystical experience. As a Yogi, he was already in possession of great knowledge and power. As a Spiritual healer he was a man dedicated to the relief of individual suffering through the Healing of disease and bodily injury as well as a teacher already established as a Spiritual psychic. He could look into the auric emanations surrounding a sick or a "well" person and if requested or allowed to do so, could administer that Healing or teaching which could help that person to become whole and healthy once more. He was so advanced as a healer that he could see, smell and feel the subtle reflection of a physical condition and treat this condition precisely as needed to bring about a Healing. Nearing a pinnacle of success and renown as a healer and teacher of individuals, George King was shown, by Higher Spiritual Forces, that he should detach from individual suffering and ignorance and become a healer and teacher of mankind as a whole.

It happened in this way. Ancient Masters of profound Wisdom saw a definite need for a person occupying a physical body on Earth through whom They could deliver information which mankind needed in order to escape from the ravages of a total nuclear war between the great powers—which in the 1950's was a distinct probability. The man would have to be fearless, an already advanced Occultist and Metaphysician, *totally dedicated* to the relief of human suffering and able to quickly build around himself an organization streamlined for practical Spiritual action.

The man chosen by the Ancient Masters was George King.

George King was alone in his London flat, at night, with the door locked, attempting to enter into a deep meditative state. He was suddenly startled by the entrance of another man into his room. George King immediately recognized his visitor as an Indian Swami of world renown, a great Yogi Adept who, although he had passed quite easily *through* the locked door, still caused the floor boards to creak from his bodily weight and the cushion of a chair to be depressed when he seated himself. Gently, but with absolute conviction, he began to explain the purpose of his visit to George King.

He stated that George King had been called upon by the Great Masters to prepare himself: "For the coming conflict between the materialistic scientist, who has arrived at his conclusions by the cold application of mathematics and the occult scientist who has arrived at his conclusions through the recognition that God is all."

After saying these things, the Master gave George King further Initiation into advanced Yoga techniques and stated that those people best suited to form a group of willing helpers would be brought into his orbit. Shortly thereafter, the Swami departed as he had come, by walking *through* the locked door!

Shortly thereafter, George King received further instructions from the Elevated Masters and, abandoning all other ambitions and interests, founded The Aetherius Society—an international Metaphysical Order dedicated to world Service through practical Spiritual action—which he still heads today. This Order has grown to embrace an active membership on six continents entirely devoted to world Peace and Enlightenment through selfless Service to mankind.

The next 22 years were an uphill fight to arouse the public mentality as well as the scientific mind against the dangers of atomic experimentation, as well as to convince mankind that we are all responsible for world conditions. The writings and teachings of Doctor George King and The Aetherius Society were a clear call for the ordinary men and women of Earth to take practical Spiritual action against the swelling tide of materialism in the world. Hundreds of books and other publications, thousands of lectures, classes, radio and television appearances were made available to the world to stimulate and inspire man and to guide him into the most

effective kind of practical Spiritual action. Slowly it began to take
effect and now, looking back at those earlier years, it can be seen
that Doctor George King inspired the beginning of a Spiritual
renaissance upon Earth, exactly as the Ancient Masters had fore-
seen that he would.

All through those years of bringing the stirring message of the
Great Plan for terrestrial Peace and Enlightenment to the world,
Doctor King never lost interest in Spiritual Healing. Telephone
calls, telegrams and letters of appeal for Healing were given his
immediate attention and again, virtual "miracles" were seen to
happen. He gave frequent lectures and taught classes on Spiritual
Healing whenever possible and trained a corps of over 50 highly
effective Spiritual healers within The Aetherius Society to give both
Contact and Absent Healing according to the techniques described
in this book.

Now he offers for your study and application, "You Too Can
Heal," a unique book which he hopes will spread the truth about
man's virtually unlimited capabilities and Spiritual potential to heal
the sick. The Healing technique which I demonstrate in this book, I
learned from Doctor King in 1960. Since then I have been privileged
to become the instrument of some cures which, in the very beginning, I could scarcely credit were possible through myself. My first
Healing attempt, although a minor one, was successful. A few
weeks later, I was amazed and humbly grateful when a disabling
and generally crippling illness "miraculously" disappeared under
my hands. The following month, a ten year old child, who had
merely watched me giving Healing to his father, used Doctor King's
technique to completely cure his infant brother of serious influenza!
Before the year was out, the incredible Power of the Divine,
through my ordinary human frame, had healed a malignant tumor!

Doctor George King knows, from years of experience, that the
techniques in this book will also work for you and that some of you
can become great healers, beginning a wonderfully rewarding
Spiritual life dedicated to the relief of the pain and suffering of
your fellow men. He knows, too, from experience that Spiritual
Healing can be a way of life itself or the first step toward even

greater accomplishments in the Service of God.

May God Bless you and crown your Spiritual Healing efforts with success.

Reverend Charles E. Abrahamson.

PLATE 2

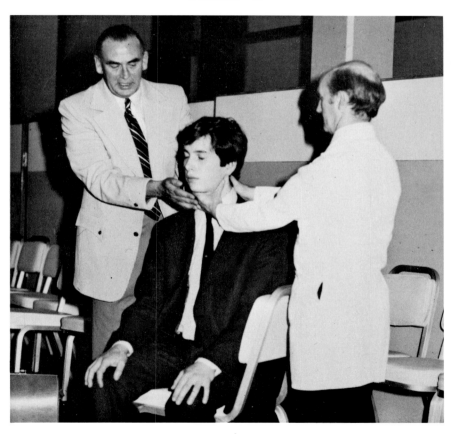

Doctor King on the public platform in the Bloomsbury Centre Hotel in London, on July 27th, 1974, demonstrates the technique to the audience while a skilled Spiritual healer, well versed in his technique, actually gave a Healing treatment during the demonstration.

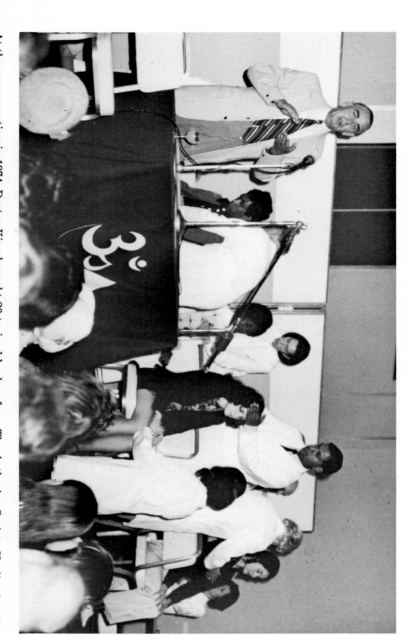

PLATE 3

At the same meeting in 1974, Doctor King brought 20 trained healers from The Aetherius Society Healing band on to the platform and while he answered questions from the audience, the healers gave treatments to everyone who desired it. About 60 members of the audience took advantage of these free Healing treatments and most of them reported great benefit from even the first Contact Healing treatment which they had ever received.

AUTHOR'S FOREWORD

The purpose of this book is not to prove that Spiritual Healing does work. Numerous healers throughout the world have proved this beyond a doubt to any serious researcher. Famous healers like Harry Edwards, from Burrows Lea in England, have been demonstrating contact Spiritual Healing from the platforms of the country in such a dynamic fashion throughout the years that this one man alone has proven to patients and the medical profession alike, that Spiritual Healing does work, very often in a fashion which defied the explanation of the scientist. Other healers, with different techniques from those employed by Harry Edwards, have also brought about astounding cures by the application of their abilities. In England, especially, Spiritual Healing is no longer a topic for ridicule, neither is it whispered about behind closed doors, but is spoken about openly and is accepted by thousands of people who have either been convinced by the numerous demonstrations from the public platform throughout the years, or have been convinced in an even surer way than this, that of receiving benefit from a Spiritual healer.

The ground work to prove the benefits of Spiritual Healing has already been laid. Therefore, the author will assume that at least most of the people reading this book will treat it as a text book, detailing a simple starting technique rather than a proof of the authenticity of this Spiritual science.

When I was eleven years old, I gave my first demonstration of Spiritual Healing!

My mother had been very ill for some time. As a matter of fact, too ill to be moved to the local country hospital which did not offer much of a service anyway, especially in those days in the very remote northern part of England in which we lived. Although, naturally, the doctor had been called and made frequent visits, he was baffled by her symptoms. It was then that he wisely suggested a second opinion, and another practitioner was called in from the nearest city some twenty miles away. As it happens, there was a delay in transportation and the second consultant could not come until the next day. As a young boy, who had been brought up in the belief of psychic phenomena, I felt, in my own adolescent way, that she was getting worse throughout the night. All local help available had been offered and appeared to be of no avail and my father was anxiously awaiting the visit of the specialist the following day. It should be remembered that all this happened forty-six years ago on the outskirts of a very small village in the north of England. There was not the speed of travelling in those days as there is today. To make a journey from the city in bad weather conditions was something not to be taken too lightly.

As time went on, I had a strange urge to at least try to do something about her condition. The urge was so strong that despite the howling wind and teeming rain outside, I left the house, climbed over a fence and walked in the pitch blackness, guided by the feeble flickering light of an oil lantern, into the woods which I loved and knew so well. I came eventually, soaked to the skin, to a little clearing where I used to play very often. When I arrived there, I had no idea of what I was going to do or even why I was there, except that I had the tremendous urge to visit this place. I set the lantern down on the wet, muddy ground and stood shivering with cold, wondering what to do next.

Then suddenly the thought struck me that I should say a simple Prayer. Although, in every way, as boisterous as any other lad of my age, I nevertheless was then a keen Church goer. Not that I believed everything I heard in Church, but something about the atmosphere of reverence I felt in a Church had a strange fascination for me. I liked to sit in the small country Church on a Sunday morning and concentrate on the light shining through the different colours of the stained glass windows. I did not look at the stained glass windows as a whole, but concentrated on the different colours of the leaded glass which made up a picturization of the Mother of Jesus or something similar. This too, seemed to give me an inner peace which was difficult to find in other places. In fact, it was the same type of inner peace which I experienced when I used to sit alone on the top of a small mountain a few miles away from where we lived.

My thoughts went to this stained glass window and I tried to visualize the beautiful greens and blues and reds of the ancient leaded lights. Then I began to pray.

It is as though the next thing had to happen.

The old oil lantern finally "gave up the ghost" and with one last puff, went out—enshrouding the whole scene in the blackness of a wet, blustery night. I felt an immediate fear arise within me, as indeed would most eleven year olds in the same conditions. However, I kept my ground and decided, come what may, I would at least say my Prayer before I left. Dimly in the back of my mind was the agonizing thought of how I would find my way back in the pitch blackness, but even that was dispelled by some basic childish courage which I seemed to invoke from deep within myself.

I started my Prayer in a weak trembling voice, which I am sure would not have carried more than a few feet above the eerie sound made by the wind as it caressed the branches of the trees, shivering as the wind blew the rain drops into my face and down my neck from a large copper beech tree some feet away from me. But Spiritual determination is greater than any other determination and this overcame my immediate desire to run—and keep running.

I noticed, as my Prayers progressed, I became braver, until at the end of saying what the Church terms as, "The Lord's Prayer," I was fairly detached from my wet, cold, dark and miserable surroundings.

I then started to pray with greater earnestness and express, out loud, the thoughts which entered my mind and at the same time tried to visualize a picture of my very sick mother lying in her bed, pale and worn. The visualization came quite easily, and when it did, I felt that instead of putting my hands together as I had been taught in Church, I should lift them in front of myself with palms facing the general direction of our house, which was some distance away from me. I found it easier to pray in this way. There was no restriction as there had been with the hands clasped together. I continued my simple Prayer, praying to God that my mother would be made well again.

And then the vision came.

Gently, at first, I became aware of a presence, unlike any other presence I had come into contact with. My eyes were tightly closed and whether I went on praying out loud or not, I do not remember. But I do remember vividly that I felt a tremendous urge to open my eyes and at first fought against it, but then curiosity or fear, or a mixture of both, took the upper hand of my shivering frame and I opened them and for a moment stared wildly at that which I saw.

Standing about ten to twelve feet away from me was the figure of a man. He had a flowing robe and long hair and seemed to be illuminated in some mysterious way from within, for he carried no lantern in his hand and yet I could see him very plainly indeed. I closed my eyes tightly and opened them again, and the Being became even clearer to my normal vision.

To me he looked gigantic, but I feel that this was part imagination and part fear. However, he was tall, with long brownish hair and wore flowing robes which seemed to be luminous in the darkness. By this time, I suppose I was shivering with another feeling besides the cold. He looked at me and smiled a wonderful, all-knowing, fatherly-type of smile which gave me an inner reassurance as would the knowing, understanding smile of a parent. He made no attempt to announce his identity, but pointed with his right hand, index finger outstretched, and simply said:

"Go, your mother is healed."

And then as rapidly as the Being appeared, he dematerialized in front of my shocked eyes and left me alone to the darkness of the storm.

I moved around quickly and kicked something on the ground next to me and almost tripped over it. It was the lantern. I searched for the handle on the top of the lantern, could not find it, and decided to leave it and make tracks for home as quick as my eleven-year legs would take me. Had it not been for the fact that I had been to this particular part of the woods very often to play and climb trees—as any healthy boys will—I think I would have been lost that night, but I knew my way home. Actually, I am not saying that I could see in the dark, but apart from the one mishap with the lantern, I managed to avoid the obstacles of the forest, like fallen trees and branches laying on the forest floor. As though I had an uncanny sight and sense of direction, I made my way right to a small ivy covered gate at the side of the old country mansion, through it and around the back door, opened it—and I knew before I did so, what I would see.

I was right.

For the first time for days, my mother was downstairs and being served food. When I walked in, she looked up, her blue eyes becoming reddened by emotion as she struggled to keep the tears from flowing. She lost the battle and they did flow; and she arose, held out her arms and held me tightly. When I could get away, I started to stammer out my experiences, although there was no need for explanations. My mother said immediately, that she knew I had gone into the woods, was praying for her and had a vision of, what she called in those days, "an Angel." When her thankfulness had died down, she ate her food and then walked, **unaided,** up the narrow staircase to her bedroom again.

The next morning the specialist arrived with our own doctor, who was dumfounded to see my mother up and preparing to mix a large Christmas cake. My mother was a very forceful, outspoken woman, and she did not hesitate to tell the doctor that where he had failed, her son had succeeded. I kept out of the way while she extolled my virtues, which were undeserved by the way, to the amazement of the two doctors. No, they did not pooh-pooh the idea. As a matter of fact, if I remember rightly, they stayed and had lunch with us and enjoyed a glass of old sherry while my mother related many psychic experiences from her childhood.

After all, they could not pooh-pooh the fact that a Healing had taken place by some means which was not described in their medical text books. As a matter of fact, more than once after that, our old country practitioner consulted my mother about other patients who were desperately ill, and together we would send them Healing and some of the results were quite startling.

That was my first conscious awareness of giving Absent Spiritual Healing. A very graphic one, far more graphic than the experiences enjoyed by most people, but it had to be that way, because years afterwards this experience, and similar ones which followed, lead me into a very close study of the different forms of Spiritual Healing. In this close study, I discovered beyond any doubt, not only what Spiritual Healing was, **but also that everyone can render Spiritual Healing services to the sick if they have the burning desire to do so.** I discovered in my later researches that what people lacked more than anything, was not the desire to help, but some way in which to **start** to give this helpful treatment.

It is for this reason that this book is written, so that all people who study it can learn a simple, safe technique, so that they can approach their friends and relatives with this technique and do so with assurance that at least if the results are not of a startling nature, which they may not be, however, some good will result from the application of the knowledge and certainly no harm can result from it.

I have taught many people this technique which has enabled them to start to give Spiritual Healing, which throughout the years has become better and better, so that today they are fine healers.

Reference to just a fraction of the case histories of The Aetherius Society, published in the back of this book, will give the reader some little idea of how this technique can be perfected in such a way as to build up within them excellent Healing powers.

CHAPTER ONE

WHAT IS SPIRITUAL HEALING?

First of all, before any attempt is made to describe a Spiritual Healing technique, it is necessary for the student to know a little about the basic science of Spiritual Healing and *why* it works. Every prospective healer should be able to answer the question: "What is Spiritual Healing?"

Very briefly, Spiritual Healing is a science in which the Universal Life Forces are conveyed from the healer into the patient.

It must be remembered that between your position on Earth and the Stars, all space is filled with Universal Life Forces. These Universal Life Forces impregnate all matter and form the matrix upon which all Creation, as you know it, is built. They come to the surface of this Planet from outside of the Solar System as well as from inside of the Solar System, and the main source of these Universal Life Forces—as far as we on Earth are concerned—is the Sun. In fact, one of the greatest philosophical concepts of modern times is a statement by an Elevated Master:

"All things on Earth are solidified Sunlight."

It is indeed a fact, with the sole exception of the main Spiritual driving force behind the brain and body of man, the Spirit Itself or, as some people might term it, the God-Force within man. This is the nearest aspect to the Creator with which we are familiar.

Man, then, is a Spiritual force, a Spark of the Divine Creative Essence, which has been thrown out from the Creative Essence Itself and has become involved in gross matter in order to learn how to control every aspect of that gross matter. Before he can complete the journey back to his Source again, he must have complete mastery over every aspect of matter and know **all** the secrets of the Universes. The journey is long indeed, spanning countless trillions of incarnations, both in this Solar System and in other Systems more elevated and beyond the one in which we now

exist. The Spiritual Aspect within you is controlling you the soul,
you the brain in all its aspects, and you the body in all its aspects.
In other words, you have built for yourself a complex machine
which you steer through material life and which you sensitize to
such an extent that you can receive and translate mind impulses into
an understandable form, and by doing this, you learn and progress
or become ignorant and retrogress, whichever you choose to do.

**This one realization alone will tend to make more difference to
your life than any realization to date.** You will appreciate, much
more clearly, the part you play in life and, vitally important, your
interrelationship with other life forms around you. The Ancient
Masters have stated that all life is One expressing Itself through
multitudinous forms in order to gain experience **of** and control **over**
matter. No truer philosophical concept has ever been expressed, for
this surely must be the basis of all logic. No other explanation of
life which is conceivable by man can be nearer to the Truth than
this, neither can it be more logical, and as Truth and logic it will
stand forever, whether accepted now or not.

Truth is. Whether it is believed does not make the slightest
difference to its existence.

The governing factor, the Spirit, is controlling its robot-like
outer form, gaining experience, in order to control through understanding the journey back to the Godhead from which it came. Like
a basic life form, a plant, mankind always reaches upward for light
and, like the plant, without this light he will wither and have to
start another journey in another body until eventually he, even
though but dimly, realizes that he must reach ever upwards, strive
ever onwards, towards his own becoming—towards the realization
of his true relationship with the Essence from Which he came, and
having come from this Essence, is an integral part of It.

It is not possible for any matter to exist in less than seven
dimensions and neither is it possible for us, with the limited
frequency range of our normal vision, to see the more subtle forms
of matter, even though some sensitive people who have developed
their psychic vision can undoubtedly do so.

Around your physical structure you have what is termed an

"aura." This aura is outside of the body and yet is interrelated to the body through, what the Yogis call, the subtle or nadic nerve centres. The subtle nerve centres are an exact reflection of the mento-physical nerve centres and membranes which can be seen by the normal senses. Just as the basic material cellular body that you inhabit needs a system of nerves through which it can become aware of outside and internal impulses, so also does your subtle or auric body need its own nervous centre so it too can become fully aware of what is happening on the more subtle planes of existence. The two are closely interrelated, one with another, and no physical matter could exist unless it had an auric counterpart, be it a blue whale or a diamond. The more you delve into the science of Metaphysics, the more sure you are of this Truth. Nowadays, with the development of Kirlian photography, the auras of flowers, animals and man have been actually photographed and scientists are now entering this new realm of science in order to study the action and interaction of forces which they, for the first time, can see with their physical eyes on the Kirlian photographic plates. Actual shapes have been photographed with Kirlian apparatus and science has "discovered" what Masters have been saying for thousands of years; that for instance, pieces of wood put into a pyramidal shape emanate different energies from the same kind of wood built into an oblong shape. In other words, man has begun to realize that all things do have an aura and auric emanations. The next obvious step science will take is to isolate some of these emanations or radiations so that they can better be studied and perhaps—understood.

What the Metaphysician says today, the scientist "proves" tomorrow!

It was known by the Wise Ones, thousands of years ago, that the Universal Life Forces impregnated all matter in Creation. That as far as this Planet is concerned, these Universal Life Forces emanated from the Sun, the Moon and other bodies in space close to us, but the major source was the Sun. The Ancients referred to them as "pranas."

There are five major pranas and five minor pranas. A major prana flows for a period of 32 minutes and then is replaced by another form which flows for another 32 minutes throughout the whole five aspects of prana. In the meantime, the five minor pranas also flow for 32 minute periods and they are inter-blended into the major pranas, so as to support all life as we know it. If you amalgamate the pranas together in one way, the result must be a piece of lead. If you amalgamate the pranas together in another way, the result would be a gold nugget; even in a different way, the oxygen in the air you breathe; a different way still, the chlorophyll which makes plant-life green.

So it can be seen that the five major pranas and the five minor pranas are not only flowing consistently throughout the day and night in and *through* all life forms, but are also absolutely vital to all material life forms. The pranas, like all other aspects of Creation, exist in a seven dimensional framework and they too have their more subtle aspects. Pranas blended in one way, help the cells in your body to continually reproduce; blended in another way, they help the cells in your aura to continually reproduce. Just as you have to put the right fuel in a diesel engine to make it operate, so also must you feed the right fuel to your physical structure so that this can exist. And do not forget—so that *you the controller* can exist within it.

The body of man has several ways in which it can be fueled: breathing, drinking and eating. If you go without breath for a few minutes, your body will die and you, the mind and Spirit, will have to leave it. If you go without drinking for a few days, the same thing will happen to your physical structure; without eating for a few weeks, again the same thing will happen to it.

From this we can deduce that while these three intakes of energy are absolutely essential to our existence in a physical body, that of the three, breathing is the most important energy intake. In fact, the Yogis say that your Karmic pattern, when you came to Earth in the present incarnation, was governed by so many in-breaths and so many out-breaths. If you take these in-breaths as short quick breaths, as most people do, you will not live as long as if you make them long and deep, retaining the energy within the body as long as possible before expulsion of the toxic matter which leaves the body through the out-breath. Anyone who has practised Yoga deep breathing exercises diligently for a few years would be apt to agree with this statement. For you not only breathe in oxygen, nitrogen, etc., which constitutes the air, but also you breathe in the essential Life Forces, or the pranas. When you drink liquids of any kind, you take in the pranas as well. If these liquids are poisoned, you will die. If they are health-giving liquids, they are essential to your physical existence, and exactly the same applies to food. (Author's Note 1.)

Just as your physical structure needs a balanced energy intake, so also does your auric structure. Unlike the physical structure though, the aura does not breathe as such, does not drink as such, and does not eat as such; and yet it does take in and expel energy and toxic materials rather in the same way as you do with the out-breath and eliminatory canal system.

You could ask: "If the aura has no teeth, how can it chew?" It cannot chew, because it does not need to. The aura takes in and expels energy through little floodgates or power vortices in different parts of its body. These are referred to as "Chakras" in Sanskrit, or as "psychic centres" in the English language.

Reference to the drawing will show you the positions of the nine major psychic centres. Each one of these has a different function, uses different energies for different purposes. But the total amalgamation of this energy intake and output is absolutely essential to material existence. Were it not for this, you would have to vacate your present structure and Reincarnate again, after having chosen suitable parents which would provide you with the experiences essential to your next life. Reincarnation is a logical fact and not theory. (Author's Note 2.)

It is not my intention in this book to go into a deep explanation of the exact functions of these psychic centres, save to say that if anyone of them is in anyway inhibited by damage to the aura, to the subtle nervous systems, or even the physical nervous systems, then discomfort or "dis-ease" results. Some "dis-eases" start within the physical body and are reflected out into the aura. Some termed "psychosomatic diseases" start in the aura or the psychic centres and have their *reflection* in the denser cellular structure of the physical body.

Some expert healers, who are able to see the aura, can make a very exact diagnosis of a physical ailment by seeing its outward *reflection* in the subtle bodies or in the incorrect working of a psychic centre. Medical science tends to study the effect, namely the *reflection* in the physical body and treat that effect without always being aware of the cause, which may quite well be a "psychosomatic condition" started by contamination or damage to the aura. Wrong thought patterns will also effect the aura in such a way as to cause a psychosomatic condition which can adversely effect the physical body.

It is absolutely vital to harmonious existence that man does not harbor thoughts of murder, greed and hate; as his thought-forms, generated by negative emotions such as these, contaminate the aura and actually inhibit the ebb and flow of subtle forces through the highest centres, namely: Crown Chakra, Christ Centre, Throat Centre and Heart Centre, and in this way his aura gradually becomes ossified and incapable of letting through energies of the highest Intuition. If these thoughts are held for long periods, then his energies begin to fall below the Solar Plexus Centre, and so contaminate the aura, that disease is reflected in the physical body.

Let us never forget, that it is the auric body we inhabit when we pass away from the so-called physical planes. If any of you have visited the hells, you do not need me to tell you what happens to the auric bodies of a murderer or a drug addict; they are warped, bent, twisted and filled with disease because they have been ill-treated in former lives when the life forms were physical structures.

Whereas the average person, with good intent and good motives, has a purer auric body and can, at death, pass away to a plane higher than the physical plane of Earth and there await his Reincarnation and another life span through the Karmic classroom called Earth.

So we have man the Spirit, controlling man the soul, controlling man the mind, controlling man the body; and all this enclosed in a subtle envelope which is a reflection of all of his thoughts and actions. The subtle envelope leaves *with* him at death, for it could be stated that that auric body with its psychic centres and complex system of subtle nerves is the *true body of man.* The dense physical body is made up of energy which he has formed into a usable shape so that he could gain experience in this for his intimate contact with dense matter.

So man the Spirit, man the soul, man the mind, in its three major forms, superconscious, conscious and subconscious, leave man the body at death. The coarse physical body slowly breaks up and is gradually amalgamated back again into the Universal Supply of Nature's Forces. But auric man lives on to be born again and again upon this Planet, until he has learned sufficient lessons here, when then he will start his incarnation on the higher physical planes. (Author's Note 2.)

It is because of the intimate interrelationship between the aura, the psychic centres, the subtle nerve centres, the physical nervous system, and the physical body, that makes Spiritual Healing so successful.

"Dis-ease" or discomfort is brought about by some wrong function of either the mental or physical workings of man, or the workings of the psychic centres. Even so, if the psychic centres all worked perfectly as they should, then even a malignant disease such as cancer would be removed from the physical body by the impingement of subtle forces upon its molecular and atomic structure.

Therefore, one way to treat "dis-ease" or discomfort is to bring about a harmony and a balance through the psychic centres into the aura where it *must,* by the Law of Nature, have its reflection in the physical body.

Hence, the evolution of my simple Healing technique, that of treating the subtle bodies so that *reflection* of this treatment will take place on the physical plane. You do not have to be psychic or a diagnostician to be able to give my Healing treatment successfully; because, as you will see in the next chapter, you treat every major psychic centre in turn and thereby bring power and balance to it.

Picture yourself as a Spiritual being controlling your complex

mental, auric and physical structure; that through your aura, great
forces are entering in a subtle state and impressing the brain of you
so that it can receive and translate mind impulses. You have complete control of all these forces and if you need more of these forces
to perform any function, you can immediately call on them by deep
breathing, by attracting them to yourself by the right thought,
whether that thought be unexpressed or expressed as it is, for instance, in Prayer or Mantra, and you can make yourself into a
veritable power house. So powerful, in fact, that you can afford to
give this life energy to one less fortunate than yourself who is
suffering disharmony, discomfort or as most people call it—
disease.

It is entirely up to you how seriously you want to help your
relative or your fellow man, as to what effort you expend as a
healer in order to charge your subtle, mental and physical bodies
with these great Universal Life Forces which are yours for the
taking. If you are serious about Healing, than you will want to eat
the right foods, drink the right liquids, breathe in the right manner,
contemplate in the right way, so that you can build up your energy
reserves; not for your personal benefit alone, but for the benefit of
suffering mankind. And by doing this, you too must progress very
greatly as you are performing the greatest Yoga known to man on
Earth today—that of Service to others.

And another thing, your Healing power will not only be
restricted to humankind, but you can dispense this freely to lesser
life forms, such as pets, injured birds, even a gold fish and a plant
will be receptive to such Healing ministrations. In fact, my experience in the past has often been that animals react far quicker to
Spiritual Healing than do some humans because they do not erect
any barriers against it. As a matter of fact, some animals seem to
enjoy it so much, that when you stop the Healing they will let you
know quite forcefully that it is your duty to continue it.

Remember the question: What is Spiritual Healing......?

Remember the answer: It is a science in which the Universal
Life Forces are conveyed from the healer to the patient.

Outside of you now, from the surface of this Globe way

beyond the Sun, is *your* storehouse of tremendous natural forces. Bring these into yourself and then you can greatly help your suffering brother.

It is your duty to do so.

AUTHOR'S NOTES:

Note 1. Read "Contact Your Higher Self Through Yoga" by George King, D.D., for a simple system of carefully balanced breathing exercises which **will** enhance your Healing powers. Published by and obtainable from The Aetherius Society.

Note 2. Read "Karma And Reincarnation" by George King, D.D. This book is unique in that the author not only describes the main aspects of the Divine Laws of Karma and Reincarnation, but also gives to the reader hitherto unrevealed knowledge of the astral spirit and higher realms. He draws from his vast experience and intimate knowledge of life on the other realms after death, as a valuable lesson to the serious student. (Ready late 1976.) "Karma And Reincarnation" is published by and obtainable from The Aetherius Society.

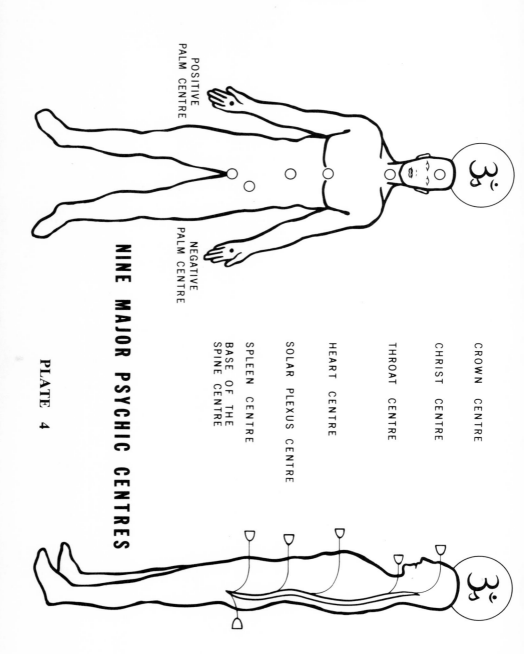

POSITIVE
PALM CENTRE

NEGATIVE
PALM CENTRE

CROWN CENTRE

CHRIST CENTRE

THROAT CENTRE

HEART CENTRE

SOLAR PLEXUS CENTRE

SPLEEN CENTRE

BASE OF THE
SPINE CENTRE

NINE MAJOR PSYCHIC CENTRES

PLATE 4

CHAPTER TWO

HOW TO START

You will never become an effective Spiritual healer unless you have:

1. Deep feeling for those who suffer.
2. Faith in your own ability.

Let us briefly examine both of these attributes so that you can learn how to enhance them within yourself.

When sickness strikes at home, many people feel gravely concerned because a dear friend or a relative may be suffering. But the same people, strangely enough, have no such empathy with their neighbours or a total stranger. This lack of feeling is one of selfishness and no matter what magnetic or Spiritual powers you possess, you will never really become a successful healer until you have almost as much feeling for the suffering of a stranger as you have for a loved one. This may sound like an impossible feat and for most people in their present incarnation it would be, unless they develop their feeling and concern for all suffering no matter who the sufferer is. Those people who have not had a day's illness in their lives are, in some ways, fortunate and in other ways less fortunate than the majority of people who at one time or another have suffered accident or sickness. It is only when you have suffered yourself that you can have understanding, feeling and compassion for others who are suffering. It is very difficult for persons to be compassionate for the suffering of others when they have not experienced suffering themselves.

Suffering is in no way a punishment, but is a great teacher. If you did not suffer pain as a child when you put your finger in a flame, then you would not learn, in a very forceful manner, that it was wrong to do so and you may, without realizing it, permanently damage your hand by burning it badly.

It should be remembered that we all exist under an all-pervasive Law of Karma. The Master Jesus explained this beautifully when He stated:

"As you sow, so shall you reap."

The Lord Buddha, talking to a more intellectual audience, said of Karma:

"Action and reaction are opposite and equal."

As a man lives this present life, so will he either progress or retrogress in the next life.

Those people who are suffering from disease today, such as cancer for instance, are people who by their actions either in this life or a former life, have brought about this negative condition within themselves. The gross misuse of your eyesight in one life, for instance to kill, will result in partial or complete blindness in the next life. There is no way that you can get around this Law of Karma for it is all-pervasive and one of the great aspects of the Divine Creator. It is perfectly fair and just to all living things, unlike the laws of mortal man. And being a Divine Law, it is absolutely a necessary one in order to keep the whole of Creation functioning in harmony and balance. Even though disease and accident are brought on by wrong thought and action, either in the present life or a former one, this does not relieve us from the responsibilities of helping our fellow man to bear his Karmic burden. Neither are you, by giving Healing to a sick person, interferring with his Karmic pattern.

I have always said that Spiritual Healing can cure all diseases, but not all patients. It is a knowledge of the workings of the Law of Karma which has brought me to this conclusion. I read the case of one of the most prominent Spiritual healers in the world whose greatest friend died in his arms of meningitis; the next day a total stranger came to him suffering with the same complaint and was cured. It is a fact that all diseases will respond to Spiritual Healing, but not all patients; it all depends on the Karmic pattern of the patient at the time, as to whether or not he will answer at all, or in the degree that he benefits from these treatments. But the idea expressed by certain schools of thought that because a man is suffering he has brought that on himself, therefore he should be left to suffer, I regard as an evil thought which should be replaced by a more positive, compassionate thought that, although he has brought this condition on himself by wrong thought and action at sometime or another, it is up to me to do what I can to help him through his misery and to go even further than that, to help to relieve the condition. Without this kind of outlook and empathy for one another, no one can become a successful healer.

It is not always a question of whether you like to give Healing treatments or not. One of the most famous healers in England, in latter years, detested giving Spiritual Healing, mainly because he felt so inadequate. So deep was his compassion for suffering mankind, that he wanted to heal everyone with a wave of the hand; but soon discovered he could not do so, soon discovered he had his failures, which at first out-numbered his successes. However, he felt that whether he liked to do it or not, he had to and he became an outstandingly good Spiritual healer. So, you should try to develop in yourself the right outlook on Spiritual Healing and you must have compassion and feeling for the suffering of others.

Faith in your own ability is essential to success. To have too much faith in your own ability is wrong. To have too little faith in your own ability is wrong. To have just enough faith in your own ability is correct. This is the balanced approach which can only come with experience. But it will come if you work towards this goal of balance within yourself.

Remember, that every man, woman and child on Earth is capable of giving Spiritual Healing. I believe it to be the birthright of all sentient beings, this ability to give Spiritual Healing to another. In fact, I will go even further than this, I believe that some species of animals, without even realizing what they are doing, do give one another Healing as a natural instinct. I have already stated that the whole Universe is filled with vibrant and essential pranic energies and these pranic energies can be controlled by you and given through you to another who, because of sickness or accident, is incapable of the same control of the energies that you are. After all, there is no mystery attached to Spiritual Healing, it is purely the conveyance of energy from the healer to the sufferer. You can write a million words about it and still say no more than that one simple, straightforward, truthful sentence.

Remember this: have a balance in the faith that you have in your own ability, have compassion for the sufferer, start off with the right technique as given herein, and everyone of you **will be able to give successful Spiritual Healing!**

I should give a warning here, which seems on the face of it obvious, but may not be so obvious when you come face to face with it. That is, do not a''ow yourself to be disappointed by apparent failure. If any healer tei s me that he has never had a failure in Spiritual Healing, then I would tell that man that he has never had a success either! You will have your failures. There are cases that you will work really hard on, that you will pray over really hard, and insignificant results will be seen. There are other times when you will give Healing and the results will be amazing.

I remember in about 1957, after a meeting in the Caxton Hall, London, England, I asked people to come up for Spiritual Healing. About forty people came forward, and myself and one or two more healers started to work on these patients. We were giving Contact Healing and adopting the same technique as outlined herein, except that I had evolved the technique to better suit my own abilities through years of previous experience. One man came forward who was suffering from a large hump on the back. I will never forget it. He was smartly dressed in a brown tailored suit, obviously made by a good tailor who had actually tailored the jacket around this natural deformity. I asked the man how long he had had this and he said, "Since birth." Making it approximately fifty years. Also, he had received medical opinions and an operation was out of the question because of the dangerous effect it would have on his spinal column and nervous system. So, he had to carry this deformity through life. I put my hands on the growth and much to my shocked amazement, **I felt it physically shrink beneath my hands!** Needless to say, all other activity in the hall stopped, because other people witnessed the "miracle" which was taking place before their astounded eyes. That man, in front of more than a hundred witnesses, got up in a dumfounded, bewildered manner, and when he walked down the aisle between the people, his jacket, which had been tailored for the deformity, **hung down like a pouch between his shoulder blades!** He was so bewildered, he did not even stop to thank me, but walked out of the hall and I never saw him again.

I was absolutely amazed at what had happened. It was the right Karmic moment for that man to be healed—and he was healed! What was most amazing to me was the fact that, when I laid my hands on the deformity, I did not feel any extra power seeming to go through them into the body of the patient. I had the same feeling of power flow as I have experienced many times in the past and no more than that.

I remember another case where someone was suffering acutely and I tried everything that I knew in the book, as it were, and brought about only a modicum of relief. The second case was not nearly as complex as the hunchback, and yet one was successful and the other only very partially so.

Another case is interesting as it puts an entirely different complexion on the science of Spiritual Healing. I was lecturing at a convention in Oregon, U.S.A., when a woman running the coffee stall had a bad fall and was knocked unconscious. I was immediately called, rushed over to the woman and brought her around. Her knee seemed to be badly injured, so I gave a Healing treatment for it and for her head as well. She was walking in a few minutes and asked the person running the convention what I had done. When she was told she had been given a Spiritual Healing treatment, she was heard to say quite loudly:

"My God, I have never had such a wonderful experience in my life. If that is Spiritual Healing, I think I shall fall down again."

She had not heard of Spiritual Healing until this time, neither had she, naturally, ever received it. The whole treatment to her was so pleasant that she described what happened and there is no doubt that she had enjoyed a mystical vision while the Healing was going on—for the first time in her life. I was at that convention all that day and all the next day and the woman was still working behind the coffee stall without pain throughout the whole of that time.

When asked about a medical examination, she "pooh-poohed" the idea, although I did strongly advise her to have a checkup on the knee to see whether there was cartilage damage. Whether she did this or not, I do not know, although I was quite forcible with my advice. Which brings me to another point.

Because you can give Spiritual Healing successfully, you should not under any account advise your patient not to seek out correct medical advice and examination. Never have I done this, in fact, the opposite sometimes; **I have insisted that people had medical attention, even surgery when necessary!** While they are having the medical attention, the Healing can still go on and can be very successful, even while the patient is in the hospital. If someone falls down and breaks his arm, it will have to be set properly. He will have to go to hospital for X-ray and have correct medical attention and there is no doubt about that at all. And anyone reading this book should remember that the medical man has his place as well and there are times when his treatments are essential. It all comes back to what I said previously; to have a balanced faith in your own abilities. To have a balanced outlook on the whole subject. If your relatives need medical attention, then they should receive correct medical attention; and while they are receiving this, you can still give your Healing, whether they are at home or even in a hospital undergoing surgery. As a matter of fact, in the Absent Healing section of this book, you will read how tremendously valuable Absent Healing can be after surgery.

Get these points fixed correctly in your own mind and then you are ready to make a good start in Spiritual Healing.

The next preparations to make are obvious ones. In raw Nature, the strong take from the weak; but in the science of Healing, **the weak take from the strong.** If you are Spiritually weak, then you cannot give Spiritual energies to another who may be suffering and is Spiritually stronger than yourself. So therefore, you must prepare yourself as a channel for a flow of these natural forces through you. The more Spiritual your outlook, the better the power will flow and the purer it will be. Do not forget, that the Healing power is coming through your aura, subtle nervous system, physical nervous system and body, so it will be "coloured" by you. Therefore, you as the healer, should be as clean in thought and deed as is possible for you.

Eat the right foods, without making a fetish of it; drink the right liquids, again, without making it a fad; and breathe in the right way; pray in the right way; have the right outlook; have a balanced faith in your own ability; and you are then able to take an important step towards your success in this Spiritual science.

The answer to a question which must have been formulated in the minds of people who have carefully studied this book so far, should be dealt with at this stage. You may want to ask: "Is there a way in which I can test my Spiritual Healing power before I treat a patient?" The answer to this question is: Yes, in part. Unless you are quite an advanced clairvoyant, you will not be able to test the *quality* of your Healing power. But even though you have no clair-voyant powers at all, you can test the strength of force of your natural magnetic output which acts as a carrier-wave for the more subtle blends of forces which make up the whole of your potential as a healer. The only real way for the average man to test the *quality* of his Healing power is to give Healing. But the "pressure" of your magnetic power can be very simply tested in the following way.

Stand about two feet away from a large mirror in which you can plainly see the upper part of your body—face and head. The cleaner the mirror is, and strangely enough the better the quality of the reflective surface, the better this test will work for you. Put your feet together and stand erect and extend your right arm in front of you with the palm of your hand a few inches from the mirror. The fingers should be spread apart and held up straight.

Now *think* Healing energy through yourself and out from the palm of your hand, at the same time try to feel what is happening to the hand. When you can physically feel a slight tingling sensation on the tips of your fingers and a very slight warmth over the palm of your hand, then very slowly move your hand away from the mirror until you arrive at a spot where you are no longer aware of these sensations. Then try the same test with the left hand. Then try the same test again, but this time with both hands extended in front of you, palms facing the mirror and move the both hands away until you can no longer feel the impingement of forces which cause a tingling in your fingers, because they are your own forces being reflected by the mirror back into your hands again. If you are powerful enough to have to take several steps back from the mirror in order to get out of the area of impingement, then your natural magnetic power is good.

If you are able to solicit help to further the scope of this experiment, get someone to measure the distance between the palms of your hands and the surface of the mirror with a tape measure. Make a note of this distance with great care. Any time in the future you can make the same test upon yourself and you can see whether the distance decreases or increases. If the distance *decreases,* it means that you are out of tune and need some exercises which will revitalize you. If the distance *increases*, then it means that the pressure behind your natural magnetic flow is becoming better and better. Even three or four inches increase will signify considerable improvement. As you give more and more Healing, you will find that this distance will increase. But in the beginning, if you can honestly feel the impingement on the tips of your fingers and a slight warmth in the palms of both hands up to a distance of 20 to 22 inches, then your magnetic flow is above the average; probably enhanced by Prayer or other Spiritual practices you have been doing. A good healer can easily increase this distance, especially at certain times of the day and year, to several feet.

Caution! It is only fair to state here that imagination can play a prominent part and you can *imagine* that you still feel this impingement which, by the way, is extremely subtle and delicate at quite considerable distances. You should remember that you are only deluding yourself by not controlling your imagination in this respect, and no one else.

This test should be confined to the privacy of your own home, but there is another test you can make in public without attracting much attention to yourself.

Gently cup the four fingers of the left hand, then push the left thumb out straight. Take hold of the thumb of the left hand, *gently* with the fingers of the right hand. Wrap your fingers *around* the thumb so that the tips of your four fingers and right hand thumb contact some part of the left hand thumb. This is important. Then say your favorite Healing prayer silently to yourself and afterwards think down the Healing power along your right arm, down through the tips of the fingers of the *right* hand into the thumb of the *left* hand. If the Healing power is flowing through you in a good *quantity,* you will feel warmth in the elbow of the left arm. This warmth will gradually increase until you feel a tingling sensation in the left elbow and the muscles around it. This is caused by the Healing power being sent through the left thumb up the left forearm to the elbow which is bent, thereby causing a restriction to the flow of your magnetic power which, I repeat, acts as a carrier for the more subtle aspects of Healing energy. If you notice a definite sensation in your left elbow after holding your left thumb, in the prescribed manner, for 60 seconds, then you may depend on it that your Healing power is flowing very strongly indeed. If after another 60 seconds, you feel the warmth and tingling sensation described, then your magnetic power is flowing very strongly and you can convey your Healing energies into a patient. If, after approximately two minutes, you feel no sensation in your left elbow at all, this will indicate that you are depleted or "out of tune" as it were. If you notice this, then try to push the energy through with your mind. If you still cannot feel a sensation, then your magnetic energy is not flowing strongly and if you have a choice as to whether you should give Spiritual Healing at that time—you will have to make the decision for yourself.

You should practise this little test at home in privacy so that you become used to the sensations caused by the purposely made restriction to the flow of your own magnetic powers and the Healing energies which they carry. When once you become used to these sensations, you will be able to detect them quickly and surely. Again, the same caution must be repeated: do not allow yourself to be deluded by your own uncontrolled imagination because this will only result in deluding yourself and no one else. You must be particularly honest with yourself.

In these ways you can always make a quick test of the force or, if you like, *output* of your inherent magnetic energies even though this does not give an indication as to the *quality* of the other subtle and higher frequency pranas which use your magnetic powers as a carrier. I repeat, the only way to test the *quality* of your Spiritual Healing power, is by the *results* obtained from the treatment of the sick.

There are several lessons published by The Aetherius Society which will help you in these respects and give you a greater knowledge and a deeper appreciation of the wonders of Creation, as well as help you charge up your own body by the correct art of the all-important breathing. (Author's Note 1.)

PRACTICE OF THE PRESENCE

This Mystical Practice should be thoroughly learned, practised and used before your Healing session begins and at the end of your Healing session, because it will, as well as raise your consciousness, help to clean any contamination from your own aura which has been picked up from your treatment of the patient. If you do the Violet Flame part correctly, you will become so impregnated with this power that you can transmute conditions which you have taken from your patient by the application of the main Healing technique.

Stand up, with spine straight, head held erect and your arms down by your sides with the palms flat against the outside of each leg. Close your eyes and make the following visualizations.

Think a vibrating, pulsating White Light down through your brain. *Feel* the whole of your brain vibrating with this dynamic, magnetic charge. When you really experience that feeling, then visualize a Golden Sphere just above the top of your head and request, with open-minded *belief,* that the Golden Ray of Spiritual energy impregnates your mental and physical and auric bodies right down to the Heart Centre. Then think *up* the transmuting Violet Flame through your feet and legs, through your physical and auric bodies, and bring together the three great Powers in the Heart Centre and visualize them as moving upwards, right above the top of the head into the Golden Sphere. Hold this visualization for a minute or two and then you should say a Prayer of thankfulness to God for these cleansing and protective Holy Powers.

Treat this Practice with the utmost reverence, for as you practise it, it will become more and more powerful within you; to such an extent that you will feel the effect it has on your Healing. Do not teach this Practice to anyone, for the more you teach it, the more power you will lose. If anyone wishes to learn this Practice, then they can go to the trouble of ordering the booklet from The Aetherius Society called: ''The Practices of Aetherius.'' If they are not interested enough to do that, then they do not deserve to know about this Practice as it would do them no good anyway. One always has to be careful about giving a powerful, Mystical Practice like this to non-believers unless they are willing to expend some effort themselves to learn about it. This is the correct and professional approach to adopt.

After this, all you really need in the way of physical equipment is a white cotton coat, which must always be kept spotless, by the way; a bowl in which to wash your hands before and after every Healing; and a stool upon which to sit your patient, if possible, kept only for this purpose; and a quiet place with subdued lighting. If you want to use coloured lighting, then green is the best. Gather these few essentials together and you can make a start by using my basic technique, for it does not demand any psychic abilities whatsoever in the beginning or the ability to make a diagnosis.

Caution: In certain states of America, it is against the law for any Spiritual healer or Faith healer to make any diagnosis of a patient and this law should be strictly adhered to. It should be noted that in some states it is against the law for anyone who is not ordained as a Minister of Religion to lay hands on a patient. It is up to you to find out the law in your state and strictly abide by that law. As stated in the Introduction, this book is not published with the idea of making you a professional practitioner, but so that you can, under certain conditions, give relief and help to your close associates and to your relatives.

If you are not sure of your legal position regarding the laying on of hands, then you can use the same technique, but by holding the hands away from the body in the aura, even though it will not be as effective as actual Contact Healing. If you again are not sure of your legal position and wish to give Healing to a stranger, then you can adopt the Absent Healing technique given here, without any nearness whatsoever, because, if you do it correctly, distance is no object.

But despite this rather stringent law as influenced by medical interests in America, I personally would not allow any authority to stop me from giving this Healing treatment to my own wife or children in my own home.

In England, Contact Healing has been given for years from parlor to public platform and providing the healer does not recommend, *which he should never do under any account,* that the patient should not have orthodox medical treatment, no law has been invoked against these demonstrations. It seems that some people in America have to wake up to the startling truth that they have allowed one of their God-given rights to be taken away from them by a few people in powerful authority.

AUTHOR'S NOTES:

Note 1. Read "The Nine Freedoms," for a deeper appreciation of the journey through vast realms of experience towards the Divine Source from which all things come.

Also read and practise "The Twelve Blessings," as given through the author by the Master Jesus as an extension of His Teachings while on Earth. The Prayers from "The Twelve Blessings" have been proved to be very effective in scores of cases of Spiritual Healing in the past. Learn and use these in your own Spiritual Healing treatments.

Regular practise of the breathing exercises contained in the book, "Contact Your Higher Self Through Yoga," will enhance the flow of the subtle forces of Spiritual Healing through you.

All these books are obtainable from the publishers.

CHAPTER THREE

THE TECHNIQUE

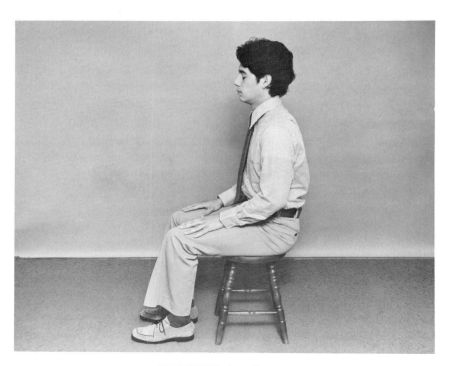

ILLUSTRATION 1

Sit the patient down in a quiet room with subdued lighting, preferably facing east. The healer should remove all rings, bracelets and watches from himself and request that the patient does likewise. If the patient wears glasses, request that these be removed as well. It is best to use a stool for the patient. If a stool is not available, then get them to sit sideways on a short-backed wooden chair, because, as you will see, you will have to have access to the back and sides of the patient.

Before starting, the healer should wash his or her hands very thoroughly in hot water and finish up with a good rinse in tepid water. In fact, hand washing facilities should be close at hand, as healers must wash their hands in clear cold water before going from one patient to another. This is very important.

If you want to use coloured lighting in the room, then green bulbs are the best. It is not necessary to have the lighting too subdued, you will have to see what you are doing.

After invoking Healing power by the use of deep breathing, Prayer or Mantra, you then approach the patient and ask them in a quiet voice where the pain is. Wherever the pain is, the whole technique should be followed very closely, as described and illustrated, with particular concentration on the painful area.

After ascertaining where the painful area is from the patient themselves, and after you feel that the power is flowing through you, then approach the patient in a definite, sure manner, so to give confidence to the patient that you know what you are doing. Make **seven passes** across the forehead of the patient and right down the back with your two hands close together, ending the pass at the base of the spine by throwing off any auric condition your hands may have picked up, as per illustration 6. This movement should be light and yet fairly quick and sure at the same time. Always keep in mind that the positive centre in the middle of your right hand gives out energy, and the negative centre in the middle of your left hand *tends* to attract that energy given out by the right hand centre back to itself again. In other words, you are working with two subtle instruments; one which gives off Healing energy and the other which "tends" to attract that Healing energy to itself, thereby causing a flow between the two psychic centres in the palm of each hand.

With some women, this polarity is reversed, but you will gradually learn this from experience. Actually, it does not really matter whether it is a right-left polarity or a left-right polarity, as with this technique, being as complete as it is, the energy will still flow in the way that it is supposed to as you will discover by further study.

These passes are most important because, if done correctly, they will:

1. Stimulate the nervous system of the patient and tend to charge it with your Healing power.
2. You will tend to pull away adverse conditions from the aura of the patient.

That is why it is essential to keep your hands close together and then throw off any condition you pull away, by moving both hands **away** from the patient in the same direction. If you feel a cool clamminess on your fingers you will know that you have pulled away a condition and make sure that you shake this condition from your hands, which is only held by the light magnetic attraction of the psychic centres in the hands, by the way, and can be shaken away easily, **if done immediately.** In other words, make sure that you throw off any condition that you may pick up from the patient. And make these passes in a determined and strictly disciplined manner, throwing off the adverse condition in **one spot of the room only,** making absolutely sure that it is not thrown back onto yourself again or that it is not thrown onto another patient who may be waiting.

After some practise at this, some of you will actually **feel** the condition and be able to throw it off quite easily and also you will be able to "see" this condition clairvoyantly as you throw it off.

Some healers do this technique of the passes so well that they have to move one hand over the other to throw off the condition, just as they would if they were ridding their hands of soap suds or mud.

When you do this, try to do it behind the patient so as not to alarm or insult him in any way. After all, if you were the patient and the healer pulled an unpleasant condition from your aura, you would not like it if the healer went to great lengths to tell you how unpleasant it was. Treat your patient with understanding and compassion, in the same way that you, as a patient, would like to be treated.

During this time, do not hold conversations with your patient or anyone else. As a matter of fact, you should only talk to the patient during the Healing when it is absolutely necessary to do so, i.e. asking questions about their pain or general condition. Do not continually make suggestions to the patient saying, "Now I have pulled that off, you will feel better." This is a Spiritual Healing technique, not a healing by psychological autosuggestion. Adhere to the advice given later in this book regarding healer-patient relationship.

All the time you are making these **seven passes**, visualize yourself as filled with Healing energy and this energy going **into** the patient. **Visualize the Healing energy as a pure, white, vibrant power.** Do not colour it in anyway. It should be a white coloured energy and you should visualize it as such. Not blue, red, or any other colour except white, this is very important for deep occult reasons.

It is also important that during these passes, the patient should sit relaxed with eyes closed, with their hands on their legs, palms down and fingers spread slightly apart as in the illustrations. This tends to hold the Spiritual power in the body that you have put in with your passes. As far as possible, this same posture should be held by the patient throughout the whole Healing.

Readers should follow the illustrations and the text very carefully as both have been specially designed to help you understand the Healing technique. The illustrations show the Reverend Charles Abrahamson demonstrating every move of this Spiritual Healing technique in such a way that the reader cannot make a mistake with it. Illustration 21 on page 74 shows the Reverend Charles Abrahamson giving Healing to a patient assisted by his wife Ellie Abrahamson as a helper.

Illustration 22 on page 90 shows Ellie Abrahamson adopting the correct standing position to send out Absent Healing. The reader will notice that the illustrations of the Healing technique have been numbered from 1 to 22 in order to provide an easily understandable reference to every mode of this Healing technique.

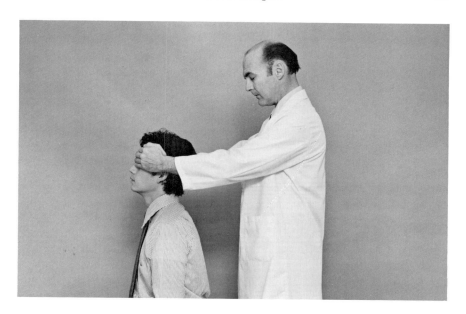

ILLUSTRATION 2

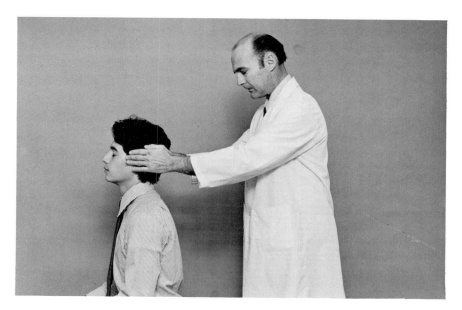

ILLUSTRATION 3

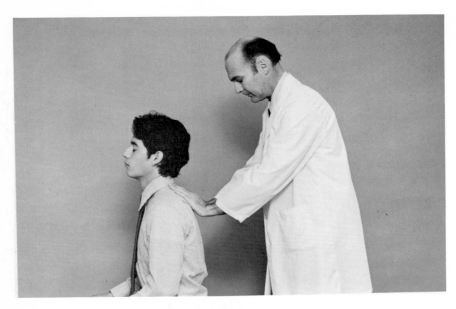

ILLUSTRATION 4

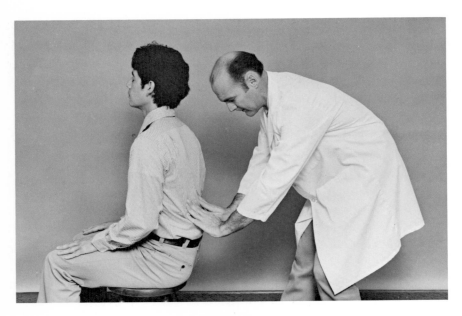

ILLUSTRATION 5

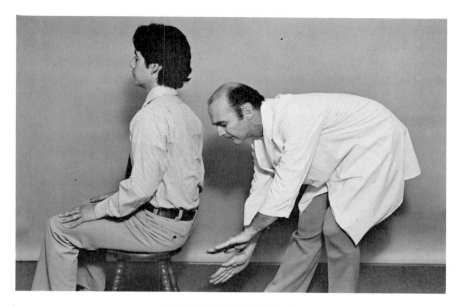

ILLUSTRATION 6

SPECIAL NOTE:

Each one of these **seven passes** should be performed in a continuous, smooth movement. Do not do these jerkily nor stop in the middle of the pass while you alter your position. With some practise you will be able to perform the passes firmly, quickly and surely for they form an important basis to the treatment.

You should start off with your hands flat against the patient's head as in illustrations 2 and 3. In the position shown in illustration 4 you will easily be able to keep your hands flat against the shoulders of the patient but when you move further down the back, as in illustration 5, you will find it easier to move the **palms** of your hands away a little but you must keep firm pressure on the finger tips.

Each of these seven passes must have contact with the body of the patient **right down to the end of the spine** and only after the end of the spine has been passed should you move your hands away as in illustration 6.

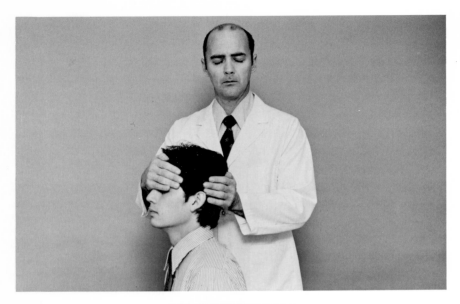

ILLUSTRATION 7

The next step is to stand to one side of the patient and then you should hold your right hand over the forehead and the left hand immediately opposite, over the back of the head, making sure to have palm contact throughout this procedure. As you do this, you should visualize a **white** power leaving the palm of the right hand and travelling through the head of the patient into your left hand. Visualize the whole of the brain of the patient being charged by this vibrant **white** light.

Hold this position for a minute or so and when you feel impressed, then move to the other side of the patient, reversing the hands, i.e. putting the left hand over the forehead and the right hand on the back of the head immediately opposite to it, and visualize the **white** light leaving the palm of the right hand and travelling through the head of the patient to your left hand. The better you do this, the better your visualization is, the more success you will have from it.

If you lose your visualization, keep your hands where they are and quickly say to yourself a Prayer, at the same time taking a few deep breaths in and out, which procedure should bring your concentration back to your visualization again.

It is important to be able to hold the visualization of the **white** light travelling from one palm of the hand to the other through different parts of the body of the patient, as you will see when you proceed further with the technique. In the beginning you may have to correct yourself as your concentration wanders, but it is all a matter of experience which comes with self discipline and practise. Students have found that Prayer is beneficial to them because it helps them invoke the Healing power in such a way that they can *feel* the power surge through them as they are giving a treatment and this also enhances their visualization at the same time. If you also perform some controlled breathing exercises such as inhaling the breath **slowly and silently** through both nostrils and exhaling it **slowly and silently,** you will find that your concentrative powers are immediately enhanced because on every breath that you breathe in you take in the Universal Life Forces with the breath.

Naturally you can perform another practice, providing it is of a high Spiritual nature, with which you may be familiar in order to control your concentration so that you can hold it throughout this technique where specified. (Author's Note 1.)

Remember—practise makes perfect!

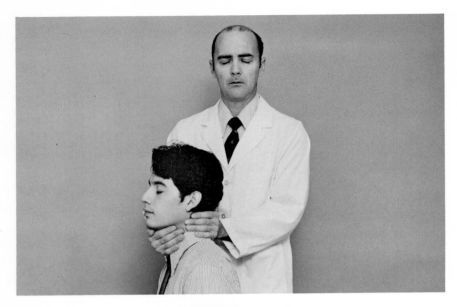

ILLUSTRATION 8

The next step is to move your position again so that you can put your right hand over the throat of the patient and your left hand over the back of their neck, again visualizing the **white** Healing power travelling from the palm of the right hand through the neck of the patient into the left hand. Now, you can also move your visualization so that the **white** light also charges up the whole head of the patient, as you did in the beginning.

Hold this position for a few minutes and then move to the other side of the patient and reverse the hands, again visualizing the flow from the right hand, which will now be at the back of the neck, into the left hand which will now be over the throat. And again, visualize this energy rising up and charging the whole head of the patient; ears, eyes and brain; so that the head is charged with this Spiritual power.

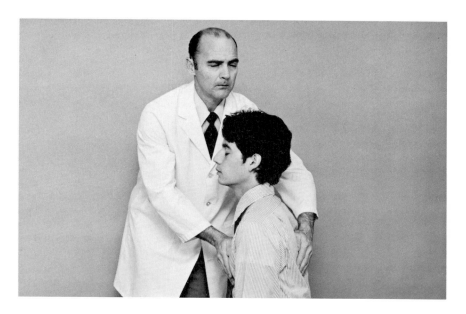

ILLUSTRATION 9

Next, move your hands down over the equivalent of the Heart Centre, which is not over the physical heart itself, by the way, but just about the beginning of the main chest bone, and your left hand opposite this in the back, again holding the visualization of the energy as a white light flowing from right to left, and this time, move it upwards by visualization and to the side, so that it impregnates the physical heart, nerves, blood, throat and head of the patient.

After holding that position for a few minutes, reverse the hands as you did with the Throat Centre.

ILLUSTRATION 10

The next step is to put the right hand over the Solar Plexus region and the left hand on the back opposite the centre as shown in illustration 10. Use the same visualization, but this time try to visualize the power travelling upwards through the inside of the body, up through the neck and into the ears, eyes and brain of the patient. After a few minutes, reverse the hands and continue with the same visualization.

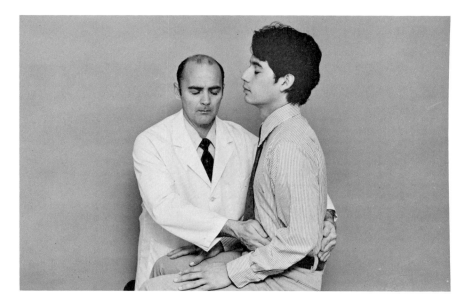

ILLUSTRATION 11

This time come down slightly **below** the spleen area with the right hand, and the left hand as near to the base of the spine as possible. Visualize the energy running between the hands, as usual, but again this time, try to visualize it rising up through, not only the whole of the body, but also going up the spine to the head and curing all ailments as it does so. This is the most difficult visualization, really, because now you have to make your energy travel through the trunk of the body, which will need some practise before you can do it correctly. But again, practise makes perfect.

After this, reverse the hands, putting the right hand as near to the base of the spine as possible, and the left hand in the front and a little lower down than the spleen, and adopt the same visualization.

Now you have given a general Spiritual Healing treatment to the patient and after this then you can concentrate on specific areas.

It is only after completing all the previous steps that you now start to concentrate on specific areas of discomfort.

Let us assume, in your preliminary talk with the patient, you have been informed by them that they are suffering from a pain in the shoulder, making movement painful. You have already asked them if they have had X-rays for this and they assure you that they have and assure you that no bones are broken or dislodged.

Move to the side of your patient as per illustration 12, putting the right palm of your hand on the front of the shoulder and the left palm of your hand on the shoulder blade behind it, and again visualize the white light travelling through the body of the patient from the right palm to the left palm. Do not send this energy anywhere else in the body as you did previously, but localize it in this one particular area.

After a few minutes, reverse the palms as you did previously, this time sending the energy from the right palm over the shoulder blades into the left palm over the front of the shoulder. Hold this position for a few minutes and then ask the patient to hold out their arm and, with the both hands cupped around the arm, make some passes all the way down the arm, throwing off the condition as you did with the first passes. (See illustration 13.) Make sure that you throw the condition into the same place as you did the first time and in this way it will be localized for a short time anyway. Make these passes quite definitely. If you do these correctly, you should be able to throw off an adverse condition which **must** have its reflection in the aura of the patient, because of the fact that they are suffering from a pain in the shoulder. Do this with precision and strict self-discipline, believing in what you are doing, and you will find that it will work for you. Like all aspects of Spiritual Healing, the better you do these passes, the more sure will be the results.

Depending on the apparent severity of the condition are the number of passes. If the condition to you seems to be very severe, then do at least **21 passes** of this nature; if not so severe, then **14** should suffice. (See illustration 13, 14 and 15.)

If the patient complains about any other centres of discomfort, you can adopt exactly the same procedure as you did with the shoulder and the arm.

In the case of the solar plexus region, for instance, the passes would be made to the side, throwing off the condition in the same place as you threw off the condition in the first passes of the technique.

Assuming then you have dealt with all the steps in order as given and also specialized on the areas of pain or discomfort as described, you can then take the finishing steps.

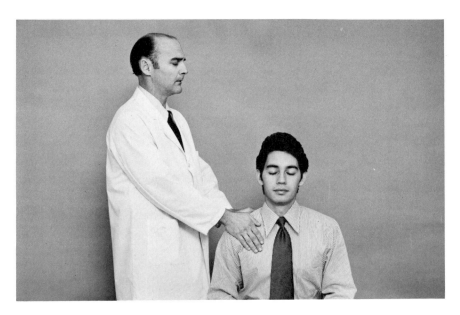

ILLUSTRATION 12

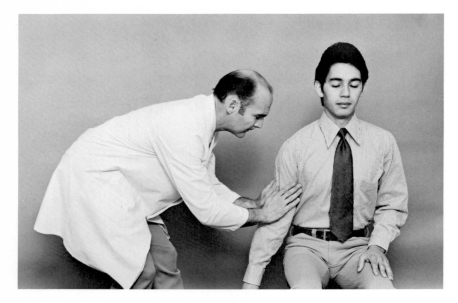

ILLUSTRATION 13

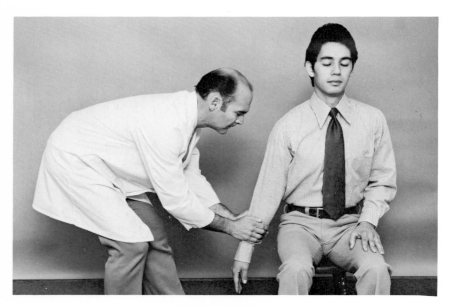

ILLUSTRATION 14

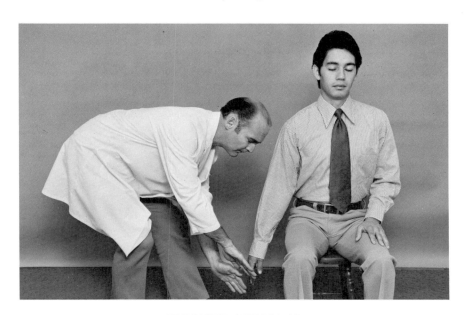

ILLUSTRATION 15

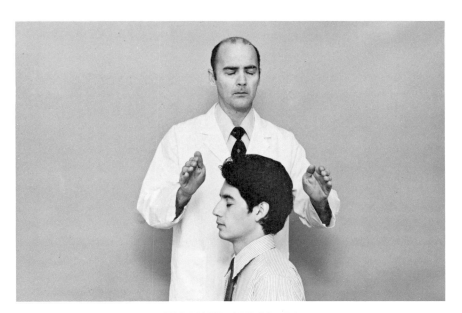

ILLUSTRATION 16

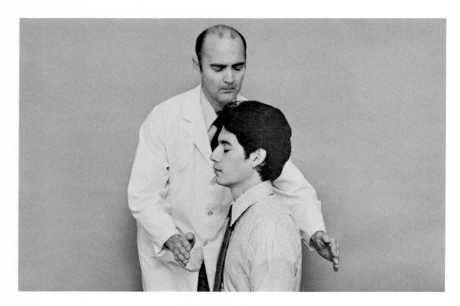

ILLUSTRATION 17

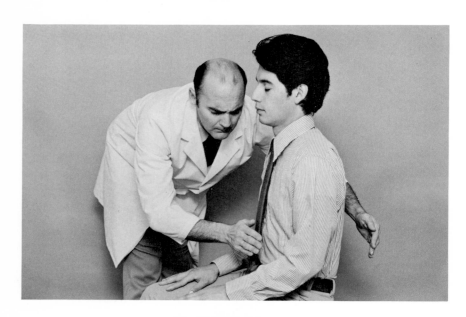

ILLUSTRATION 18

Stand near the patient with your hands above their head and making sure that the power is flowing through you, as shown in illustration 16. Then move your hands **close** to the body of the patient, as shown in illustrations 17 and 18, all the way down right to the feet. In this way, you are putting the last charge into the aura of the patient. You must move your hands **all the way around** the patient, trying to visualize the vibrant white Spiritual Healing power leaving your hands and charging up their aura.

This is also done for another reason. With the Healing, you must have, to some extent, caused slight, which may be termed as, **"ruffles"** or **excess pools** of energy in certain parts of the aura of the patient, and these have to be smoothed out, and they can be if you try to visualize the aura while making sure that you pass your hands **all the way over it as much as possible.**

This procedure is more difficult to explain than it is to do it. I have never had any student who has not caught on very quickly to this explanation and they find that they can do it after a little practise quite well. But do make sure that you move your hands in such a way as to travel over as much surface of the aura as possible.

ILLUSTRATION 19

After you have finished the treatment, the patient should be asked to leave the Healing chair and then you should "clear up the mess," so to speak. You have pulled away conditions from the aura and from painful parts of the patient, and the etheric matter is still laying there on the floor where you deposited it, so now you must transmute it. This again is not nearly as difficult as it seems to be.

Hold your hands above the position where you threw off the condition and practise the Violet Flame Practice as given in the last chapter. You should visualize this Violet Flame as coming through the whole of your aura and thereby cleansing it for you, and also streaming from your hands and transmuting any adverse etheric condition which you threw off. While you are doing this, concentrate on the Healing chair or stool and send the Violet Flame over it and *through* it so that no condition from the last patient remains on or in this furniture.

When you feel sure that you have cleared up the condition, then you should make certain that you wash your hands in cold water before you continue with the next patient.

Do not even shake hands with your last patient, or naturally the next one, until you have washed your hands in cold water kept in a non-metallic basin, which should be somewhere in the vicinity **but not too near** to the actual Healing stool.

A light wash of the hands is all that is necessary at this stage, as water will clear any subtle condition from your hands which may be remaining. After you have washed them, then dry your hands on a clean cotton towel which should be laundered regularly.

Then you are ready to bid goodbye to your last patient and go on to the next one if this is applicable.

This washing of the hands in cold water after **every** Healing treatment is an essential part of the technique and a step which should not be forgotten by the healer.

If you have finished Healing for the day then you are ready to take the next step in this technique—which although very simple is extremely important to you.

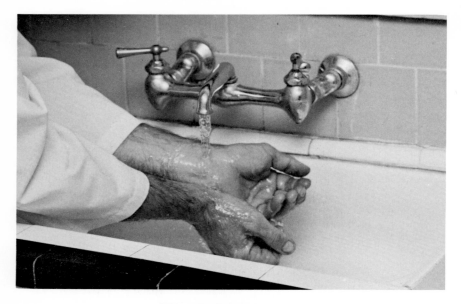

ILLUSTRATION 20

If you have finished Healing for the day, then wash your hands thoroughly in cold running water, ending up by running water for about a minute over the **insides** of both wrists as per illustration 20. This will cut off the power flow from you so that you will not waste your valuable Spiritual energy. Make sure that this is done properly and the flow of Healing power has stopped before you dry your hands.

Then take off your Healing smock or white coat and hang it away in such a place where it will not get dirty or be contaminated by other clothes. If there is the slightest feeling in your mind that it may be contaminated by the conditions of your patients, then throw it into the washing machine. This Healing smock or coat is important and should always be kept scrupulously clean. If in any doubt, have two or three of them so that you have spares while one, which has been in use, is being washed and dried.

You have just performed a complete, perfectly balanced, absolutely safe Spiritual Healing technique. The more you practise it, the better you will become at it and the better will be the results. Do not try to modify this or miss any of the steps, as they are all put there for a very good reason and are the results of years of research into the science of Spiritual Healing.

AUTHOR'S NOTES:

Note 1. There is some excellent advice on the control of concentration on the Cassette No. C-7 called "Concentration, Contemplation, Meditation," a 90-minute lecture given by Doctor George King. This Metaphysical lesson will help you to make great strides forward in Healing. Published by and obtainable from The Aetherius Society.

CHAPTER FOUR

HEALING WITH A HELPER

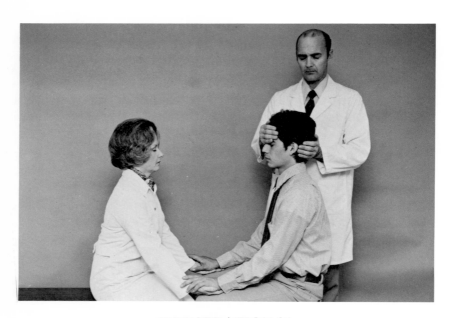

ILLUSTRATION 21

You will find that when you start Spiritual Healing, many people will want to come and help you in this humanitarian undertaking. You should insist that any helper purchases a copy of this book, "You Too Can Heal," and reads it thoroughly before you accept their help. Do not lend them a copy, because if they are not interested enough to procure their own copy and thoroughly study the technique for themselves, then such a helper would not be much assistance to you anyway.

Let us assume that a friend, just as humanitarian as you are, wishes to help you in giving Healing treatments. Can they do so? The answer is definitely "Yes." If the friend is of the opposite sex from yourself, this will be more beneficial from a purely magnetic point of view. But if of the same sex, then by all means accept their help. Either way you should make sure that they have carefully studied this technique, *from their own copy of this book,* and that they know what they are doing before you *allow* them to help. This may seem a little hard to you, but I speak from years of experience, not only my own, but from those of my students as well.

The procedure will be exactly the same as that outlined for the single healer, except that the helper will sit down in front of the patient, as per illustration 21, and instead of the patient laying their spread hands on their own legs, the helper will take their hands in his or hers, laying palm to palm. While you are going through every step of the procedure as outlined, the helper will visualize his or her Healing power running through the palms of the patient's hands and right through **all** parts of the patient's body. This can be of tremendous help to the patient, as you can see, in that they are being charged with, not only your energy, but that of your helper as well.

You may also find that after working together with a helper for some time that they seem to obtain better results than you do with certain ailments. This has happened many times in my experience. If so, then you go through the procedure as outlined and let the helper take over for the concentration points, such as the shoulder that we illustrated here. Meanwhile, you take the patient's hands and continue pouring in the Healing power through the palms of their hands. A combination of two dedicated healers working together like this can be of tremendous benefit for the patient.

You should be careful though that your helper is as interested and keen on giving Spiritual Healing as you are, for if they are the **weak link** in the chain, they can actually sap your energy from the patient and thereby leave the patient depleted as a result. You are the only person who can make this assessment and you should do so with the **thought of your patient in mind** and not be swayed by relationship or friendly feelings towards any helper.

Always keep your goal in sight and never lose thought of it.

You are there to give Spiritual Healing, not to show friendliness to a relative or an acquaintance. You have ample opportunity to do this outside of the Healing Sanctuary.

You may think these to be unnecessary words, but believe me, they are very important ones. I have had many years of Healing experience and have taught many people to perform this technique, and it is because of this past experience that I speak in the way that I do.

Notwithstanding these pitfalls, if you make your judgement correctly, you could find that you have a fine assistant, probably an ex-patient, as I have discovered that many times when a patient is healed of a complaint by a Spiritual healer, such is their relief and gratitude that they wish to give Healing themselves and wish to be taught correctly and to assist suffering humanity in every way. A helper such as this often becomes a very good one indeed, for they can feel for others and have confidence in Spiritual Healing because it has either cured them or brought them considerable relief.

So choose your helper wisely and educate him or her correctly, and together you can form a Healing partnership which could be of great benefit to your patients.

CHAPTER FIVE

SELF HEALING

During my numerous public lectures and public demonstrations of Spiritual Healing, the question always arose: "Can I heal myself?"

The answer to this question is: "Yes you can."

It is essential for a Spiritual healer to enjoy health which is as good as possible and therefore it is his duty to look after his own health so that he remains magnetic and dynamic enough to be able to pass Healing energies on to others. If you are depleted, then most often your Healing treatments of others will be poor. Also, you will notice that some people are Spiritual energy "vampires" and will sap your energy from you. I have dealt with this subject elsewhere in this book.

If you need self-Healing and you do not know anyone who has studied this technique sufficiently well to give you effective Healing, then give the Healing to yourself. In some cases, it will not be as effective as receiving Healing from another person, especially if they are a good Spiritual healer, but you can do a great deal for yourself by:

1. Adopting the correct mental approach.
2. The correct diet.
3. The correct exercise.
4. The correct breathing.
5. By short-circuiting the Healing power within you so that a concentration is made in certain parts of the body which need vitalization and "ease" in order to drive out the "dis-ease."

The technique for self-treatment is a simple one and, of course, depends on the seriousness of the condition suffered by the healer. If it is a serious condition, then do not hesitate to seek professional medical, osteopathic or chiropractic treatment, whichever is necessary. If the condition does not seem to be serious enough to warrant orthodox professional help, then you can often help yourself greatly by adopting the major points already given, together with the following simple technique.

Start your self treatment by standing up, facing east and performing the mystical "Practice Of The Presence" as outlined in Chapter Two.

Then lie down full length on a comfortable couch or your bed, in a quiet room away from traffic and fumes, of course. Then lay the right hand, palm downwards, over the solar plexus region. Lay the left hand, palm downwards, **on top of the right hand.** This will tend to enhance the flow of the Healing energy through the nerve centres, especially concentrating it in the solar plexus region which is a very important battery for the human body. Then breathe deeply in a measured count, holding the breath for half the time of the inhalation and breathing out for the same count as the inhalation. The rhythm should be: 2-in, 1-hold, and 2-out.

While you are breathing in, visualize the prana flowing into the body with the in-breath. While you are holding the breath, which must be done without imposing any strain on you, visualize the prana as a brilliant white light filling your body from head to toe. While you are breathing out, visualize all the toxic materials leaving your body with the out-breath. **Do not put any other colour on the breath, only a brilliant white.** This is very important in the early stages. (Author's Note 1.)

After you have done this for approximately a dozen breaths, then continue with the same breathing rhythm, but this time, while you are breathing in, whisper to yourself, "Great peace, great peace." Try to *feel* your whole body becoming relaxed and filled with deep, harmonious, relaxing peace.

When you are relaxed, remain in the same lying position without moving, with the right hand palm downwards over the solar plexus region and the left hand laying lightly, palm downwards, upon the back of the right hand as previously stated. This will tend to lock the energy flow in the body and also charge up one of the main basic nerve batteries of the body, namely the Solar Plexus Centre.

When you feel a peaceful condition within your whole body, then placing your left hand over the Solar Plexus Centre and while continuing with a deep in and out breath, hold your right hand over your forehead. Visualize the pranic Healing power flowing from the psychic centre in the palm of the right hand down through your body to the Solar Plexus Centre where your left hand is. After a few minutes, move the right hand down and lay it over the throat, *making sure that the centre of your palm contacts the front of your throat.* Then, move it down to the Heart Centre, the same position as you learned in the technique of Healing others. Now move the right hand and lay it over the Spleen Centre. Then put the right hand on the solar plexus region and duplicate the whole process with your left hand. You will not easily be able to hold either hand over the base of the spine or the back, but frontal treatments should bring good results, providing your visualization is as good as it should be.

Now, with the tips of the fingers of *both hands,* gently *brush* as much of the body as you can reach, starting from the top of the head, down the face, etc., with the *tips* of your fingers, while thinking to yourself that Healing power is entering you and making you fit and well. Do this brushing at least 21 times.

Now, let us suppose your pain is in the left shoulder, then put the **left hand** on the solar plexus and give treatment into the shoulder with the right hand as you would in the main Healing technique. If the pain is in the right shoulder, then reverse the position of the hands.

If the pain is in the legs or knees, you may have to sit up on the bed to give Healing to these spots. If you do, then lay the right hand over the front of the painful part of the leg and the left hand on the back of it for a few minutes, and then reverse the hands.

Try always to hold the visualization of being filled with vibrant, white Healing power which is driving the condition of discomfort from you.

After you have done this, then lie flat again and take the

measured, slow in, hold, slow out, breaths without any strain whatsoever. It is up to you to work out for yourself what suits you best in this respect, but the rhythm of 2-1-2 should be adhered to. Then relax the whole body. I know that this is far easier said than done, but a few tips from the ancient science of Yoga should help you to do this. Lay the hands alongside the legs and, believe it or not, **tighten up every muscle in the body as hard as you possibly can!** Really use effort in doing this, and then slowly—ever so slowly—relieve this tension until you have no tension whatsoever in the body. At first you may have to do this tightening exercise at least three times before you can obtain the desired results. But as one who has practised Yoga diligently for many years, I know that sooner or later this technique will help bring on a condition of deep relaxation. Oddly enough, it is a tip which few teachers seem to know anything about.

Then relax completely.

Starting from your feet, relax them. If there is any tension there, move them slightly. Try to get the tension out of the feet and gradually, mentally work all the way up the body, part by part, internal organ by internal organ, and relax it—until you are **completely relaxed.**

Another ancient occult practice here is when you get to the heart, think first of all a great love for your own heart. You will, after some time, feel a response from your heart; then gently, delicately, with great love, feeling and compassion, ask your heart to relax, but to beat slowly and strongly. This will help to bring about a relaxation throughout the whole body. Above the heart, the throat and the eyes, the ears and the head and, of course, the neck. Continue this until you are completely relaxed.

It has been stated by Yogi Masters that 15 minutes of complete relaxation done in the right way is equal to five or six hours of normal sleep, and I would agree with their findings in this respect.

You will discover that the first time or two you try to relax it will be difficult, for all manner of thoughts will enter your mind. But gradually as you practise more and more, then you will become more and more proficient at it. It is in this state of deep relaxation that the Healing power which you have put into yourself will have a chance to bring harmony and ease where dis-harmony and dis-ease were making themselves painfully known.

After 15 or 20 minutes of relaxation like this after your self-Healing, then *slowly* bring yourself to activity. In other words, do not suddenly leap off the bed, but *slowly* bring yourself back to normal activity again, arise from the bed and perform The Practice Of The Presence with special emphasis on the Violet Flame part of the Mystical Practice. When you *feel* the Violet Flame rising through you, then wave your hands over the bed, as you have been taught, to burn up any etheric condition taken off your patient, in such a way as to ensure that the whole bed and the room in close proximity is thoroughly clean. Then say a Prayer of thankfulness to God for the Healing which you have given to yourself.

And then comes one of the most important aspects of any Healing technique, be it self-Healing or Healing another—a secret known only to the few, although it is so absurdly simple. Even the Masters have kept this Mystical key as a closely guarded secret to ensure the success of Spiritual Healing or other advancement practices, but believe me it is the last stepping stone to success in either Healing yourself or another.

This Mystical key can be explained in one word—detach!

When you have given yourself the Healing treatment to the best of your ability, taking as much care as you would if Healing a loved one, and after you have cleaned up the bed and room afterwards, then **detach** from your Healing—and the results! Do not give it a further position in your thoughts. In other words, have complete faith in your own abilities, in the technique and most important, in the fact that because you requested in a reverent manner the Healing power to flow, **know** that it did flow through you. That is why detachment is so important. It is the last link in the chain. It is as though you had complete faith and were expressing this through your detachment.

Only attach yourself again to your own self-Healing or the Healing of another when you want to perform it the next time.

I will be apparently dogmatic and state that ALL healers,

whether they are in the best of health or whether they need a treatment or not can benefit themselves by this simple self-Healing technique. I also state from practical experience, that the better you can perform this technique for your own benefit, the better you will be able to give Healing to others.

AUTHOR'S NOTES:

Note 1. Read and practise the techniques given in the two specially prepared little booklets: "Contact Your Higher Self Through Yoga" and "The Practices Of Aetherius," both by the same author and obtainable from The Aetherius Society. The practise of these techniques will greatly enhance your Healing abilities and enable you to not only give more effective Healing to others, but to yourself as well.

CHAPTER SIX

EDUCATION OF PATIENT

Even though, with your Spiritual Healing, you bring about the relief or cure of a condition within a patient, this does not always mean to say that the relief or cure will be lasting. It should be remembered that the patient brought the condition on himself by wrong thought and action or neglect in any one of its multitudinous ways. Therefore, if he wishes the relief or cure that you have brought to him to be fully beneficial and lasting, he will have to change that part of his character which brought the condition to him in the first place.

It is for this reason that the healer should make some attempt to help the patient bring about a change for the better within himself. As a man thinks, so he is. This is true of anything relating to "dis-ease" or disharmony within the human mind or body. Naturally, every case has to be judged on its own merits, as every patient's psychological makeup is entirely different. So therefore, a good Spiritual healer will try to find out what big mistakes are being made by the patients and try to educate them in such a way that these mistakes can be avoided.

Although this book deals with the basis of Spiritual Healing and does not go into such areas as correct diet, however, it is assumed that those people interested in giving Spiritual Healing will learn a little about the vitamin and mineral content of foods so that they can give advice to their patients. I know some readers will take this seriously and I know that some will think that they have to be ultra-fadish about diet and pass these fads on to their patients. This is not necessary. It is not necessary, in order to be a good healer in the first place, to be a vegetarian, neither is it necessary for the patient to become one unless he so chooses. If the healer has made his own decision to become a vegetarian for health or humanitarian reasons, then he should stick to it, but not necessarily expect everyone whom he comes into contact with to follow his example. This is just put out as a very simple illustration of what I am trying to convey to you. A good, healthy, balanced, clean, nicely cooked diet, with the right mineral and vitamin content, is essential for everyone's well-being, whether healer or patient. An excess of alcohol, for instance, will put the patient back where he was before you laid hands on him in your Healing Sanctuary—is another illustration. Incorrect, shallow breathing will also tend to bring a condition back to a patient, even though you may have brought what you consider to be a complete cure. This is especially so in every mental disorder researched to date.

So therefore, it is left to you to find out as much about the patient as he is willing to tell you and if necessary, try to steer him into the right approach to the care which he should take of himself.

This is especially true of a Spiritual outlook. If your patient is a gross materialist, with no time whatsoever for anything outside of his own selfish material world, and he steadfastly holds on to these ideas, even though you have proved to him the strength of Spiritual powers, then such a patient can only be expected to retain whatever relief or cure you have brought about for a relatively short time. In this case, he must bring about a radical change in his outlook and thought in order to really benefit and enjoy a lasting cure. He should be encouraged away from his selfish ideologies, if possible and told to render some Service to humanity without any financial reward, by the way, whatever that Service may be—and there is a world full of Service to be done.

You will have cases where your patient will obviously have to have medical attention, you should not in anyway try to talk him out of this. I have known some healers who have dealt with patients under medical care who have gradually encouraged their patients to *wean* themselves from drugs which seem to be very readily prescribed by some medical practitioners today. Note, I say *very gently* wean themselves away from these drugs, not give them up straight away and entirely if their health depends on the taking of these drugs.

There will also be cases when there is skeletal damage to the patient, then you would be advised to get him to attend a good osteopath or chiropractor and one who works strictly from X-rays and one who knows what he is doing. In the United States of America, there are many good chiropractors. In fact, the most famous colleges of chiropractory are in the States. In other parts of the world, chiropractors may be few and far between. However, very often these practitioners bring relief and sometimes lasting cures to people suffering from certain ailments, especially those to do with the skeletal deformities or bones dislodged. I personally would not hesitate to recommend any patient, whom I felt needed it, to take another form of Spiritual Healing as well as my own, namely, chiropractory. And you will find that osteopathic and chiropractic treatments work hand in glove with your Spiritual Healing.

In these ways, not only is the aura and subtle nervous system helped by your Spiritual powers, but also the all-important skeleton is put into shape by a qualified osteopath or chiropractor, both of whom, if they are good ones, are extremely skillful practitioners.

Do not forget what you are trying to do. You are trying to heal by Spiritual means and you should use all other means at your disposal, such as advice to take correct medical, osteopathic, chiropractic and dietary treatments as well. After all, we all want to see our patients cured. *It does not matter who cures them—as long as they are cured!*

Before I finish this chapter, I must answer the question: "Is it right to take money for Spiritual Healing?"

There are two schools of thought on this. Some healers believe that they have every right to make a charge for Spiritual Healing as does an osteopath or a dentist, for instance. They state—and quite rightly so—that it has taken them just as long to learn and perfect their science as it would take a surgeon to become proficient. Therefore, as the surgeon is worthy of his hire, so are they. This is one definite school of thought which has its merit. The other school of thought is that it is "un-Spiritual"—whatever that may mean in this case—to make any charge for Spiritual Healing, and some people go so far as to say that under no account would they accept even a love offering from a grateful patient.

Neither I nor the other healers in The Aetherius Society have ever made a **fixed charge** for Spiritual Healing. But, if any grateful patient cares to donate towards their Healing treatment, this donation is accepted, but does not go into the personal pocket of the healer, but goes to the Society funds for the upkeep of the Healing Sanctuary. I believe that this is the correct approach to take. **After all, you cannot receive unless you give,** and this Law applies equally to Spiritual Healing. All too few patients even think about what they owe the healer. Even though some of them have been saved from very dangerous operations, they still seem to take this as a matter of course. **This is a wrong approach and should not be agreed with!** Although you are not giving Spiritual Healing for a financial reward, however, you should gratefully accept any love offering—gift—which a grateful patient feels that he **must** give to you as some practical expression of his gratitude for the relief or cure you have brought about within him. **There is nothing in the Spiritual code which stops you from accepting such a gift!** In fact, I would go as far as to say that the patient who continually receives free Healing treatments from a healer, whether he has felt any benefit or not, and does not make some attempt to give that healer something in return, is so completely ignorant that he needs re-educating.

Again, may I repeat—you cannot receive unless you give. That is the Divine Law which governs all of us, and the patient should be aware of this Law as an essential part of his Spiritual education. Nobody expects a tooth extraction or medical surgery, or any other kind of orthodox medical or psychological treatments, without having to pay for them. Yet, the same people will come week after week to a healer, tell the healer, probably in all honesty, that they feel: "Better than I did when I went to the doctor," without leaving a penny in the collection box for the upkeep of the Sanctuary. It is almost unbelievable this, but it is true. I am afraid that you as a healer are going to discover this for yourselves. Not that such lack of basic decency should stop you from giving treatment to such a selfish person, but I think there comes a time in everyone's life when straight words should be spoken and such a person should be reminded of the Divine Law—**you cannot receive unless you give.** If you lose him as a patient because you have given him a reminder of one of the all-pervasive Laws of God, then you have lost nothing except, in most cases, a time waster anyway.

One last word about time wasters. Some patients, no matter how much Healing you give them, will return for more. Some people like Spiritual Healing so much that psychologically *they keep themselves sick and in need of it.* You will recognize such a person and you will have them, especially if you gain success in your Healing. They will flock around you like wasps around a honey pot, wanting to sap as much power from you as they possibly can. You should always beware of such Spiritual energy "vampires," because such people will take power from you and no matter what your ability is, they will never, ever seem to get better from your ministrations. They will psychologically make *sure* that they are not completely cured because they have this great love of the Healing itself and of absorbing power from you.

Watch out too for the typical hypochondriac who will be suffering from so many complaints that it is really astounding that they have the strength to get up out of bed in the morning, never mind make frequent journeys to come and see you, very often through all kinds of adverse weather conditions. These people should be taught—and in some cases believe it or not it is possible to teach them—that they should keep a positive approach to life and not a negative one. Give them the following autosuggestion to use: *"Day by day, in every way, with the help of God, I am getting better and better."* Tell them to repeat that for 10 minutes in bed before they go to sleep *every night* and several times during the day as well. I have found that this autosuggestion has brought change for the better in the lives of people who before this practice were typical hypochondriacs or, if not that, had a negative, despairing approach, like persons condemned to suffer forever.

As a matter of fact, referring back to that autosuggestion, it is one which you can safely give to any patient and even use yourself as well. A conscious Truth like this, impressed enough times on the subconscious mind, causes the subconscious mind to bring into being those conditions which will make you better and better. This is a well-proven fact of applied psychology.

To sum up this patient education by the healer, it can be done by giving the patient confidence in you in a quiet manner, so that once you have his confidence, then you will find that you can help your patient very greatly, not only with Spiritual power, but with the right, positive, unselfish, balanced outlook, which will bring great changes for the better in his life. I feel that this healer-patient relationship, whether it exists between yourself and a total stranger or even yourself and a relative, is a very important part of the cure.

Again, practise and in this case, experience—brings perfection.

CHAPTER SEVEN

ABSENT HEALING

One of the great wonders of Spiritual Healing is that the Spiritual power can be directed by thought from the healer to the patient irrespective of distance. This procedure is called Absent Healing.

Absent Healing is essential when the patient cannot visit you because of distance or confinement to his own house or a hospital bed. There are several ways to perform Absent Healing, mainly dependent on conditions prevailing over you and the patient.

One method is for you to start off the Healing by adopting the contact or auric technique as described herein and then continue, because of distance or other difficulties, the Healing with absent treatments; either visiting your patient or have him visit you, say once every two weeks.

Another method is very useful where a patient is absolutely confined and the healer and patient cannot meet.

And even another method, where the patient is more mobile and of a calibre who can be taught to concentrate themselves while the Healing is being given at specific times.

Each of these procedures works very well indeed. Probably the one working the best for the average healer, especially in the beginning, would be when the Healing is started off by contact or auric treatment and then has to be continued as Absent Healing. But whichever way you adopt, the procedures are almost the same.

To send out Absent Healing, you as the healer must prepare yourself just as you would for a Contact Healing, with the same care, i.e. showering the body so that it is clean, putting on scrupulously clean clothes and your clean white Healing smock or coat, and then stand facing east and invoke the power within yourself. This is done by practising "The Presence" as outlined in an earlier chapter, doing some deep breathing practices and by Prayer. Go through this ritual in the order as given and you will soon be filled with natural Healing powers.

ILLUSTRATION 22

When you are so filled, put your arms outwards, with palms on the left and right hand side of you so that the action of the positive and negative psychic centres corresponding to the centre of each palm, is not in anyway inhibited, with your fingers straight upwards and not bent, as in illustration 22. Then you visualize a **white** light leaving the palms of your hands and—if you are able—your Heart Centre as well, and travelling **quickly** to the patient, charging them up from head to toe with this radiant Healing power; holding the visualization, at the same time, of their body and aura being fully charged with this power and them being in radiant health. If you know of any ills or deformities suffered by your patient, **do not recognize these** in the visualization as existing, but visualize your patient in perfect, radiant health.

This technique can be adopted for a patient whether they are bedridden or not. It would be beneficial if the patient reciprocated by co-operating with you, therefore, you would have to make a prearranged time and stick strictly to it, so that the patient would know when you were sending the Healing. If you can get patient co-operation in this way, it will be very beneficial to the patient. All the patient has to do is to lie or sit quietly, facing east if possible, but not absolutely essential, and allow the Healing power to flow through them. If you cannot get patient co-operation, as for instance if you are sending Healing to a patient who would put up barriers of disbelief against it, then do the Absent Healing anyway if you have been requested to do so.

Another method which has been tried by groups of healers in The Aetherius Society and proved to be extremely effective is this. They get the patient to sit or lie quietly at a prearranged time, preferably at night, looking at a blue light in front of them. The patient is concentrating on this blue light when the Healing is sent. This is particularly effective because we have the concentration of the patient directed towards the blue light and, in some cases, this allows the Healing power to flow through them more easily.

A blue light can be made up in many ways; an ordinary light bulb with a deep blue shade over it, or even better still is to use an ordinary colour slide projector and obtain some commercial gelatins—a good one is called "Cinemoid"—and just project this onto a screen as you would project a colour slide. In this way you have a good overall colour and also you can blend colours so that you can get as pure a deep blue as you wish.

Such a procedure as this, if you can get your patient to co-operate with you—and if he is suffering sickness and wants to be healed, it is up to him to help in this Healing—can be very beneficial indeed and help the whole Healing process along.

There are more advanced techniques than this for giving Absent Healing, but these will only be given by personal individual instruction to healers who have studied this book carefully and have some practise in Healing in order to prove their genuine interest in this form of Spiritual Service to others. (Author's Note 1.)

However, do not for one moment judge this technique by its utter simplicity. We have hundreds of case records on file from patients from all over the world who have been greatly benefited, some of them actually cured of both chronic and acute conditions by the simple adoption of this method of Absent Healing.

Read Chapter Nine of this book for just a few of the scores of case histories on file about the results brought about by the application of this Absent Healing technique.

It does work!

HEALER-PATIENT RELATIONSHIP
IN ABSENT HEALING

There are so many different conditions covering this, that only the very broadest outline of the healer-patient relationship regarding Absent Healing can be gone into at this stage, for every case is dependent on the conditions governing it.

But very briefly, if you are treating a patient some distance away; for instance at the other side of America, or as far as Europe is concerned, in another country; whom you have not met or not likely to meet physically, then the usual procedure is to have a written report from this patient or a relative or other person representing this patient at least every two to three weeks. This written report should state how the patient is getting on, whether any improvement has been noted or not, and very important, if the patient has to go into hospital for surgery or other treatment, you should be informed about this beforehand. If they have to go into hospital to undergo a surgical operation and you know the time of this operation, then you can make sure that you send them Healing power for at least 15 or 20 minutes **during the operation and also after the operation.**

A good procedure to adopt in this case is the following. Your patient has undergone a medical examination. The doctors are not sure whether or not they have to go into hospital until X-rays and other tests are made. The patient or relative informs you of this over the phone or through the mail. Immediately you tell them that you will send Absent Healing and make a time so that they can concentrate in one of the ways outlined above, and you send the first Absent Healing treatment for 10 or 15 minutes. After a few days, back come the reports of the test and the patient has to go for another medical checkup and to hospital for surgery. The patient should, in this case, try to inform you or have a friend do it, when they arrive at the hospital. When they are in hospital and you feel they have settled down, probably sometime during the first evening, send another Absent Healing treatment of 10 to 15 minutes. Along come the X-rays or tests and the medical consultants state that surgery is necessary. Now, if the patient can tell you the exact time of the operation, it will be extremely valuable. Let us suppose that they can do so and the time of the operation is 2:00 p.m. If it is a serious operation, **at approximately 2:30 p.m., send 15 minutes Absent Healing.**

At 5:00 p.m., send another 15 minutes Absent Healing.

At 9:00 p.m., another 15 minutes Absent Healing.

And if the operation has been extremely serious, try to send another 15 minutes Absent Healing beginning at exactly midnight, i.e. **the patient's time, not yours.**

To continue our hypothetical case, you are then contacted by a relative to say that the patient has to have further surgery. Well, again try to ascertain the time and if you can do so, adopt the procedure outlined above. If you cannot ascertain the time for the second operation, then send the Healing at 2:00 p.m., 5:00 p.m., 9:00 p.m. and midnight, as outlined.

If you are informed that the patient has undergone the second operation and is in critical condition, then put in an extra Absent Healing session at 7:00 p.m.

It all depends on the conditions appertaining to the surgical operation. But if you use the indications given as a broad outline, they can be modified to suit the times which apply to the operation. Very broadly speaking, if the operation is scheduled at 2:00 p.m., then allow about 30 minutes **before** you send a treatment.

You will find with Absent Healing that a number of short treatments are, in most cases, far more beneficial than one long treatment. Use this information for the benefit of your patient because it does work in this way.

Eventually your patient leaves hospital and is recuperating in a convalescent home. Still keep sending the treatments in the morning, in the afternoon and at 9:00 p.m., until they leave the convalescent home; and when they do so, then you can set up a time to have the patient co-operate with you in their own home, using the procedures I have already given.

In this way, you can greatly help a patient who is undergoing surgery, with hospital and convalescent home treatments following this.

So you can see that a good communication line should be established between you and an absent patient if you are to help them in the best way possible to you. Without this communication line, then your Absent Healing will be less effective because you will be working in the dark.

Again, a caution. You will no doubt receive letters and requests from friends and relatives for Absent Healing because some people feel that this is easy on them. They do not even have to bother to visit you and if you are not careful, **they will take advantage of you in this respect.** Be advised by this and do not allow **anyone, even your nearest relative,** to take such an advantage. If they want Absent Healing and they have expressed a belief in it, then the least that they can do is to co-operate with your times in the way **you** suggest and to keep you fully informed by letter or telephone every two to three weeks—three weeks being an absolute maximum time between reports. If they are not interested enough to do this, then you should not waste your time or precious Spiritual Healing power on them, because in the end you will not do them much good anyway.

I have known some Healing Sanctuaries in the past which, throughout the years, have built up a number of Absent Healing patients and diligently the healer, or the group of healers, spends time, two or three days per week, sending Healing to patients who have not even had the decency or courtesy to ask to be removed from the Healing list when they felt better.

My adamant advice to all of you is to start in the way you intend to continue and **demand** these reports or simply state that their names will be taken from your Absent Healing list. It is far better to do this **right from the beginning** than it is to suddenly try to tighten up after offering your services in an undisciplined manner for a few months. So start right and keep it right. It is almost heart-breaking to discover that there are people who have received wonderful Absent Healing treatments from The Aetherius Society and other famous Healing centres throughout the world, who have not even had the common decency to inform us when they no longer needed these treatments. But I am afraid this is another one of the blows you will get when you become a healer, a blow which you must not let affect you in any adverse way.

On the other hand, you have your legitimate patients who will keep you regularly informed. When they are better, such patients will send you nice letters of true thankfulness and gratitude for what you have done for them. These are the people who deserve Healing and this is the type of person you should concentrate on.

This book has given you an insight into the wonderful power which has been put into your hands. A power which can be given to your suffering brothers through the aura, by contact or over a distance, and it is to be hoped that a whole new world of Service has been opened for you.

You should remember that the greatest Yoga of all is the Yoga of Service, and by the administration of Spiritual Healing, you are giving a true, selfless Service to suffering mankind. You are helping him to progress as well, for your Healing power not only cures the physical effects in the body, but will often help to cure the mental causes in the mind as well, will bring the patient a greater realization of the wondrous world of the Spiritual forces. As well as this, you are progressing yourself by performing two great types of Service, namely, the Bhakti Yoga of love and compassion and the Karma Yoga of actively helping your fellow man.

By the Divine Law of Karma, you must also reap your own reward. Because by your potent Service, you will balance your Karmic pattern to such an extent that you will gain a deeper realization and appreciation of the Divinity around you, as well as a knowledge of the use of the miraculous tools contained within Nature's finer forces.

Learn.

Apply.

And you will discover that—YOU TOO CAN HEAL.

AUTHOR'S NOTES:

Note 1. Contact The Aetherius Society for information regarding advanced classes on Spiritual Healing which will be offered to students who have studied this book carefully.

CHAPTER EIGHT

QUESTIONS AND ANSWERS

QUESTION: Are we allowed to show this technique to friends?

ANSWER: No. It is best to keep this to yourself, as you do lose occult power when passing it on. I have lost a tremendous amount of occult power by showing this technique to people during public meetings. Possibly you cannot afford to lose so much power. Also, now that the book is available, everyone has easy access to this knowledge and you need not deplete yourself. After all, any prospective healer who is worthy of the name will want to purchase his own copy of this textbook and carefully study if for himself.

QUESTION: Can "spirit guides" or discarnate entities help healers?

ANSWER: Yes, most certainly! Some healers do have "spirit guides" who help manipulate their power. The guides cannot use their own power, as this would be a contravention of the Law of Karma. The better healer you are, the more these guides can and will work through you.

Sometimes too, the healer goes into trance and a discarnate entity will manipulate power through him. Sir James Young Simpson, for instance, worked through me in the early days. Also Pasteur and Lister are doctors who wish to continue with their Healing. However, this is a rather advanced Healing technique as a good deep trance condition must be developed.

It is not necessary to wait for this. Application of the technique in this book will enable you to start Healing without any need to go into a deep trance condition.

QUESTION: When a healer feels that a person would benefit greatly from Spiritual Healing, should he use strong persuasion to get the person to take Healing?

ANSWER: No, you should never do that. The patient should ask for Spiritual Healing—this is the Law. However, you may have to prompt a little sometimes, because some people are a bit shy about asking for help for themselves. If you do want to help a person and they do not want to ask you for your treatment, then give them Absent Healing, unless they definitely tell you not to. If they do, then obey their wishes. In other words, adopt a professional approach to your Healing.
Spiritual Healing is Holy—treat it as such.

QUESTION: Does the patient have to have faith in the healer?

ANSWER: No. I have found, especially with Absent Healing, that excellent results were obtained when the patient did not even know that Absent Healing was being sent. Therefore, faith did not enter into it at all. Wild animals and plants are incapable of faith in the way that we know faith, but we have seen them healed many times.

QUESTION: Is diagnosing necessary to success in Spiritual Healing?

ANSWER: With the Healing technique described in this book, it is not essential. It is sometimes helpful if you can do it, but it is not a necessary ingredient to successful Healing treatments.

QUESTION: Is it essential for the patient to face a specific direction?

ANSWER: No. Although facing east is best, this is not always possible as in the case of the patient who has to stay in bed, for instance.

QUESTION: Can the Healing technique described, be used for a patient who is in bed?

ANSWER: Yes it can, but it depends how ill they are. If they are too ill to be moved, placing the hand underneath the body could pose a problem. If you cannot put your hand underneath, then just hold your hands **over** the different psychic centres in the front of them as described in Chapter Five on Self Healing.

If the patient is in the hospital and you do not want the staff to know that you are giving Healing, then just hold the patient's hands, pushing the power right through them, visualizing it filling them completely. You can also put your hand over the patient's head or over the throat. Also, you can always continue Absent Healing afterwards, especially once you have made a personal contact with the patient.

QUESTION: Before commencing the Healing treatment, should one request to be a channel for the Holy power to flow forth?

ANSWER: Yes, most certainly. I personally always do that and also take a few deep breaths up one nostril and down the other. Learn some basic Yoga type of breathing and request that you be filled with Healing energy. Some people feel they heal better after having said Prayers. Some people say Prayers whilst giving Healing. Whatever helps you to be a better channel, to heal better, by all means adopt it. Everybody is an individual in this respect. One thing you should **not** do is to have a heavy meal just before you give Healing, because this will very often upset you. Just have a light meal or a meal a few hours beforehand. This is the best way.

Another absolute must before approaching the first patient of a particular Healing session is to perform the "Practice Of The Presence" as described fully in Chapter Two of this book.

QUESTION: Why is it called "Spiritual Healing?"

ANSWER: Somebody invented the title a long time ago, probably because they thought Spiritual powers were being used. Personally, I prefer the title "Natural Healing" because it is the most natural method of Healing in the world, but most people would not know what you were talking about if you called it that.

QUESTION: Can you give a guideline as to how long one should give individual Healing?

ANSWER: It really depends on when you, as the healer, think that the patient has had enough Healing for one session. Some patients will take a lot of power from you, others not so much. However, a broad guideline would be about fifteen to twenty-five minutes per patient.

QUESTION: How often can one give Healing to the same patient?

ANSWER: If you are a very powerful healer, then you should not give too much Healing to the patient too quickly; say once or twice weekly. If you are a moderate healer, you can give it more often, leaving a few days between Healing sessions. It all depends on the severity of the complaint suffered by the patient. Use good judgement. Study the Chapter on Absent Healing—this will give you a good idea of the frequency of Healing sessions which should be given to a patient who is dangerously ill.

QUESTION: When having made the pass over the patient and thrown a condition off, should it be transmuted before continuing with the rest of the Healing?

ANSWER: If you wish, you can do this. The modus operandi as fully described at the end of Chapter Three has proven itself effective in the past.

QUESTION: When holding the hands over the psychic centres, do we visualize the white light leaving the palms of the hands?

ANSWER: Yes. Another very good visualization is to visualize the patient as fit and well. Do not use any other colour but "white" though, because you may be using a colour which is wrong for that patient and that disease **at that time.** If you can visualize a **white** light leaving the right hand, going right through the patient to the left hand, and the entire body and aura of the patient as being infused with this **white** light, that is a good way to do it.

QUESTION: Should the patient come back for more treatment if he feels he needs it?

ANSWER: Most definitely yes. The patient does have a moral obligation towards the healer to give him as fair a chance as he would give to any medical man and he should continue with his Healing until he feels better. As a healer, you will often find that some patients have been to doctors, naturopaths, they have tried diet, they have tried just about everything, and when all else has failed they come along to the Spiritual healer. Well, no healer can put that kind of patient right in a few minutes. The patient must keep on with the treatment and not leave it after he feels a little better, for he may slip back again.
Some patients may have to have treatments for twenty times, sometimes even longer.
The patient should give the healer a fair chance. It

may take some time before any improvement is noted, but then suddenly the patient will start to get better and when this happens the patient should KEEP ON with the Healing treatments.

QUESTION: What should we tell a patient who asks if he should give up his medication?

ANSWER: Until that patient knows that he can safely give up his medication, he should not be told to do so by the healer. When the patient is better, it is up to him to give up allopathic drugs of his own accord, with the co-operation of his medical doctor. The healer should not tell any patient to give up his doctors. **That is a decision the patient must make for himself.**

QUESTION: Is it a good or bad sign when the patient goes to sleep during the Healing?

ANSWER: Each case must be judged on its own merits. When people go to sleep on a Healing couch, we are happy because it means they were able to relax completely, which allows the Healing power to flow freely into them.

QUESTION: Would it help to use gentle music while Healing?

ANSWER: If that helps you and the patient, use it. Gentle music of the right kind is extremely relaxing and it can help a Spiritual Healing treatment along.

QUESTION: Does it matter if the patient, who attends a Healing group, cannot always get to see the same healer?

ANSWER: This is entirely up to the individual. If you are satisfied with the other healers, then by all means have Healing from other healers. However, we have found that most people prefer to continue to receive Spiritual Healing from one particular healer because they have confidence in him and they like his style. In that

case, it is better for the patient to have the chosen
healer continue with the treatment.

There is an exception to this rule—that is when the
chosen healer feels that it will be beneficial for the
patient to receive Healing from another healer, just to
cause a different reaction pattern, to stir things up a
bit as it were. Often in such a case, the patient may
feel worse the next day, but will feel much better
afterwards.

However, generally speaking, if you have confidence
in a healer and you go to a group, it is better to stay
with the same healer rather than have treatment from
a different one every time.

**Keep in mind though that you can Heal all diseases
but not all people!**

It depends on the Karmic time. Some people get a
complete Healing after just one treatment, others
may have to attend time and time again—for months
even before any really substantial change takes place.

QUESTION: When giving Healing for the first time, how does one
know that one is doing any good?

ANSWER: There is one sure way and that is when the patient
tells you sometime afterwards, he feels very much
better. You will then KNOW that you have done
some good.

QUESTION: Sometimes people feel worse after a Healing. Is there
an explanation for this?

ANSWER: Spiritual Healing from a powerful healer may cause
the patient to feel worse the next day. This is an excellent sign. This means that you have stirred things
up; have started the ball rolling as it were. Generally
the day after they will feel better.

It sometimes happens that a patient receives Healing
and really thinks it is marvelous having this Healing.

This is not always as good as it may seem. It is best, in such a case, to have another healer give a treatment to stir things up and very often the patient may feel very bad the next day, but very much better the day after.

So there is no need to be concerned if you find that your patient feels nervously disturbed the day after the Healing treatment, for you will find that the day after that they may feel very much better.

QUESTION: Can the free energy flow be hampered by restrictive clothing or certain kinds of clothing?

ANSWER: Ordinary clothing does not hold up the flow of Spiritual Healing energy. However, if you wore silk gloves, you would most definitely hold up the flow of energy. It is difficult to give Healing to a patient wearing silk, because silk can pick up the energy and throw it all round the body of the patient. Pure silk is a super-conductor of Spiritual energy. It is very hard to push energy through pure silk.

The healer's white coat should be made of cotton as it does not have the same degree of conductivity as nylon. Also, cotton will not allow the absorption of contamination as do some nylon yarns. Cotton is fairly inert and it is not easily impregnated with subtle influences.

QUESTION: Could harm be done if one cannot take off a ring?

ANSWER: You **may** do yourself much harm, especially if you are a really powerful healer. Even if you are just a beginner and if one day you really hit a peak—and in your life as a healer you occasionally do so—you could have a psychosomatic condition form around a ring, because the metal, especially gold or silver, could hold up the flow of energy and could "compress" it, because this energy is "compressable," just as electricity is "compressable" under certain conditions. So be careful of this! Have your rings enlarged so that you can remove them. This is essential for other occult practices as well. So attend to this important detail straight away.

QUESTION: If the healer is below par himself, would it be advisable for him to give Healing to others?

ANSWER: If you are tired and feel depleted yourself, I would say that, in the beginning anyway, it would be best **not** to give Healing to others. When you give Spiritual Healing under those conditions, you can deplete a patient if you do not know how to manipulate power. Charge yourself up first before you give Healing. Practise the Self Healing technique described in Chapter Five of this book.

QUESTION: Does the technique in this book have any effect on mental conditions?

ANSWER: These are generally the most difficult to deal with and you will have to stay with it for quite sometime usually. However, significant relief has been given to people with various mental conditions. A person in a mental home can often be helped by sending Absent Healing to them.

QUESTION: How does one deal with obsessions?

ANSWER: This is a highly specialized field. Do not attempt to deal with any obsession cases yourself unless you are a fully trained medium in all forms of psychic self defense. If you are not, then give Absent Healing. (Author's Note 1.)

QUESTION: Is the power of Prayer with Absent Healing as beneficial as Contact Healing?

ANSWER: Not always. But the power of Prayer is beneficial for

Absent Healing. Never underestimate the power of Prayer, as it is a very potent way to invoke Spiritual power.

QUESTION: Is there anything the healer can do to prevent a condition from reappearing?

ANSWER: Some illness is brought on by certain mental conditions. If the patient does not change his thoughts and actions and continues to live as he has in the past, the condition is liable to return. He needs mental re-orientation and the healer should educate the patient accordingly. Read and practise the advice given in Chapter Six called: "Education Of Patient."

QUESTION: What steps should the patient take to repay the healer for his time and effort?

ANSWER: Any labourer is worthy of his hire and although most people do not want to do Spiritual Healing for financial profit, there is a Law which can be stated thus: "As you give, so shall you receive." So the patient should be very thankful for his cure and should, in all fairness to the healer, make every attempt to repay that healer back in one way or another.
One should also not forget to thank God for the Healing. The patient should be thankful to the One Divine Creative Source for the Spiritual Healing he has received. The healer too, should thank God for his Healing power.

QUESTION: Can you Heal yourself?

ANSWER: Yes, indeed you can. See Chapter Five of this textbook.

QUESTION: When passing through adverse astrological conditions, what can one do to protect oneself?

ANSWER: If the astrological condition is one where you are extremely susceptible to illness, you can protect yourself by adopting a positive approach to life's problems. Keep to bright, cheerful colours during such a time, that helps a great deal. Do a lot of praying and give as much Service to others as you possibly can during such a time. In this way you can transmute the—shall we say—negative aspects in your horoscope.

QUESTION: Can a woman give Spiritual Healing as effectively as a man?

ANSWER: As far as the application of the technique in this book is concerned, the answer is: Yes, providing the woman uses the same degree of concentration as the man does on the flow of Healing energy through her to the patient.

I realize that most of the prominent Spiritual healers have been men and there are many occult reasons why this is so. There are also some basic reasons for this as well. One of the basic reasons would appear to be that when some men discover that they can administer successful Spiritual Healing, they go all out and make a career of it. I think more women would make a career of Spiritual Healing if they did not have the responsibilities of bringing up a family and looking after a home.

However, there is no doubt that men and women alike can give very effective Healing by applying the carefully balanced technique given herein.

In The Aetherius Society we have approximately as many men healers as women. I think some organizations have found that they have more women interested in giving Healing than men. This is probably because some men may be, without encouragement, reluctant to try it in the beginning.

As I have stated in this book, it is my firm belief— backed up by years of experience and research—**that**

every man, woman and child can give Spiritual Healing, and I feel that it is the duty of every man, woman and child to do so!

This book was written to enable the layman to make an effective start at Spiritual Healing irrespective of his age or sex. Healers of many years experience have adopted the same technique that I have taught here and have improved their Spiritual Healing successes very greatly, according to reports we have received throughout the years. It can be said of the technique given herein, that it is equally usable by man or woman and by beginner or experienced healer alike. After all, whether male or female, you will never really know how good a Spiritual healer you are until you try it—will you?

AUTHOR'S NOTES:

Note 1. There is an outstanding series of specialized classes given on cassette tapes called "Psychic Self Defense." These cassettes deal with the essentials of self defense from psychic attack. An illustrated brochure comes with this course showing postures, and mystical hand signs, the use of which are fully described. This information is essential for ALL practising Spiritual workers. Write for free literature to The Aetherius Society.

CHAPTER NINE

SPIRITUAL HEALING SUCCESS

The main idea behind the publication of the following case histories is to give the reader confidence in the technique as described herein. These are a few of the case histories picked from the Healing files of The Aetherius Society. It should be borne in mind that none of these successes was brought about by, what may be termed, a famous professional healer, but by ordinary, Spiritually-minded people who have learned the technique described in this book from me and have carefully applied the technique, both in their Contact Healing and Absent Healing. You can read for yourself what the results are. We feel that they are very, very impressive indeed.

This will give you a good idea of what can be done by adopting the advice given in this book and by the very careful application of the Healing techniques with the right Spiritual outlook and motive.

You should read all of these case histories with great care and so build up faith in the validity of the technique as given in this book, as well as form a foundation for faith in your own abilities as a prospective healer.

SUCCESS BY CONTACT HEALING

CASE NUMBER 1.

A woman with bad eye trouble was waiting to go into hospital for an operation. She came along for one session of Contact Healing and when she went to the hospital soon afterwards, found to her amazement that she no longer needed the operation.

CASE NUMBER 2.

After a cancer operation, a woman who was found to have incurable cancer received several Healings. Five years later, she is still working in a part-time job and enjoying life. She has also remained on the Absent Healing list since then.

CASE NUMBER 3.

A man with advanced cancer had an operation for the removal of the pituitary gland. He was suffering from severe headaches when he came along for Healing and was unable to work. After only four sessions the headaches disappeared and he was able to resume work. He is still working and has had no more headaches.

CASE NUMBER 4.

A severe rheumatic pain in the knee brought a woman along for Healing. After one session, the pain disappeared and so did the limp she had. She continues to be much improved.

CASE NUMBER 5.

A man with suicidal tendencies and severe depression was given six weekly Healing sessions. Afterwards, he was much improved and was able to reduce the allopathic drugs in co-operation with his doctor.

CASE NUMBER 6.

A woman who had suffered from a stomach ulcer for two years received Contact Healing. She was also taught about the Law of Karma and learned how to send Absent Healing to her father, who was very ill and bad tempered. One month later her ulcer disappeared and did not return. Her father's health and temper became so improved that the rest of his family were amazed.

CASE NUMBER 7.

An eight year old boy with a badly sprained ankle could not sleep with the pain. He called on one of our healers and received Contact Healing. The next night he slept perfectly and called in the following morning to say thanks. He had no further pain.

CASE NUMBER 8.

A woman with back pain had not had any relief from the allopathic drugs prescribed by her doctor. After receiving Healing, the pain disappeared and has not returned.

CASE NUMBER 9.

An extremely painful knee had meant that a woman had to attend hospital twice a week for eighteen months, but she had still had no relief from the pain. After only one session of Spiritual Healing, the pain disappeared overnight. The healer reports that she said her knee felt as though it was burning while the Healing took effect. Later, to demonstrate how successful it was, she ran up and down the stairs in great excitement.

CASE NUMBER 10.

A woman who had spent three months in hospital with poliomyelitis, was released from the hospital in a wheelchair. After receiving Contact Absent Healing, she is now able to walk again.

CASE NUMBER 11.

A recently-joined Member of The Aetherius Society, eager to learn how to give Healing himself, was found by one of the senior healers to have a serious defect in the alignment of his collar bones. This had been caused by a bad accident two years before. After receiving Contact Healing the Member found—to his astonishment —that the next morning the collar bones had moved back into alignment and the slope to the left had disappeared.

CASE NUMBER 12.

A long-standing and dedicated Member of The Aetherius Society was attending a special Seminar in the north of England.

Just before the programme was due to begin, she suddenly felt ill and collapsed. Fortunately, two very experienced Aetherius Society healers were on hand and they were able to render emergency Healing to her. She recalls that she felt as though she had "passed over," and one of the healers says she did in fact stop breathing for a time. Naturally, an ambulance had also been called immediately the incident occurred, but by the time it arrived, the lady in question—although still unconscious—was breathing normally. She was not even detained in hospital afterwards, although it did appear she had suffered a heart attack. She has had no recurrence since and still regularly attends meetings.

CASE NUMBER 13.

A Member of The Aetherius Society was in Spain with a friend. The air was clean and fresh. She felt a prickling sensation in her fingers, a sign that she felt she could do Healing or Prayer, so she asked her friend if there was anything wrong physically that needed righting. The friend, who over the years had suffered from a very bad knee and had been visiting an osteopath, asked if the Member could do something about the pain in her knee which was hurting quite badly at the time. The Member made the usual preparation for Healing, then placed her hands over the afflicted part. The friend felt an acute pain for a while. Then suddenly, there was a "puff," a sound audible to both women, and with that the pain was gone—and did not return.

CASE NUMBER 14.

A Staff Member of The Aetherius Society was struck with severe rheumatism two years ago and was in considerable, constant pain with this condition from that time on. The person in question—while never allowing her condition to interfere with her Staff duties—has received a lot of Healing during this period. She has been on the Absent Healing list and has also had Contact Healing at the Headquarters. Outside help, in the shape of homeopathic and radionic medicine, has also contributed to the overall

Healing, along with expert massage from a South African Member staying in London for Society activities. In the words of the Staff Member herself: "I know that I have also been given Healing from invisible helpers." She goes on to say that now—and only just recently—she has had a tremendous improvement in her condition. This is certainly apparent to those who work closely with her all the time and have seen how difficult any physical movement has sometimes been. The Staff Member adds another significant remark: "I also attribute this improvement partly to the ownership and use of a Holy Cross which has been Blessed by Doctor George King and which I acquired recently." (Author's Note 1.)

CASE NUMBER 15.

While visiting her grandparents in India, an Aetherius Society Member was able to give her grandfather very effective Healing. He had collapsed in the house and was carried to his bed. He was very cold and lay stiff without movement. His breathing had almost stopped and his pulse was also very faint. After ten or fifteen minutes of Healing had been given, the old man began to recover. When he came around, he said to the healer that she did not know yet what she had found, but she should never let it go. He said he could feel the Healing power going through him and that wherever she had learned how to give Healing like this, she should never leave; i.e. The Aetherius Society.

CASE NUMBER 16.

A young Aetherius Society healer was at her work when she heard that someone had collapsed down in the machine room. She went down to see if she could help and saw a man lying on the ground. He was undergoing very violent physical spasms. She went over and took one of his hands in her own and began to visualize a white light going into him through the psychic centres of her palms. Suddenly the spasms stopped and he became cold and still. Everyone thought he had died—his pulse seemed to have stopped and so did his breathing. But, with **complete faith** in the power of

Healing, she carried on with the visualization for between five and seven minutes until a faint breathing could be detected and his hands started to warm up. People around asked why she was doing this and why a complete stranger's life meant so much to her; but she ignored them, except to say that the real test of Service was to give it at anytime to anyone to the best of your ability. Fifteen minutes later—when the ambulance finally arrived—the man had completely recovered consciousness. The healer adds: *"This proved to me that Spiritual Healing—even a fraction of the whole practice—does work if you have love for all people in your heart."*

CASE NUMBER 17.

The mother of a Staff Member of The Aetherius Society had fallen downstairs and had severely damaged her left leg, requiring about twenty stitches. After several weeks the leg appeared to be getting worse and severe swelling and pain was experienced. Contact Healing was given and the patient, who was sceptical, experienced a burning sensation which passed up one leg to the top of the head and down again out through the other leg. The result was the immediate cessation of pain and the disappearance of all swelling *within an hour* after the treatment.

CASE NUMBER 18.

A lady requested and was given Healing ten days prior to surgery scheduled for the removal of a cancerous uterus. The day following the surgical appointment, she called the healer to state that surgery had been unnecessary as examination had revealed a perfectly healthy organ, free of malignancy. *Her physician recommended that she continue going to her Church—The Aetherius Society—as often as possible!* (Author's Note 2.)

CASE NUMBER 19.

An Aetherius Society Member had an operation on her wrist. It was badly swollen and had a painful growth. Even after the operation, the wrist still hurt and she was given Contact Healing, since which she has had no further pain.

CASE NUMBER 20.

A woman was suffering with severe chest pains and extreme difficulty in breathing. A senior Aetherius Society Branch Officer went to see her and found she had grown very weak and thin as a result of this condition. He gave her Contact Healing once a week for six weeks and also put her on the Branch Absent Healing list. He instructed her in breathing exercises and advised her to drink charged water and sugar cane molasses as described in the book "Contact Your Higher Self Through Yoga," by Doctor King. (Author's Note 3.) In the first two weeks of treatment she reported that the chest pains had been reduced and she was breathing a little better. Within four weeks, her wheezing had stopped and she was putting on weight again. By the sixth week, she was so well and strong that she was able to go out and shop for the family. She has maintained the recovery and had no need for further treatment during the past two years.

CASE NUMBER 21.

An elderly woman with very bad back pains was given regular Healing by a Member. She later had a bad fall at her home and was taken to hospital, where the Member went to see her. While she was waiting, she was able to send Healing to the sick woman and she soon recovered from the fall. The patient now reports that the pain in her back has improved greatly and she had almost forgotten what it was like.

CASE NUMBER 22.

Two Committee Members of The Aetherius Society gave one Contact Healing treatment to a woman who was brought to the Branch by a sympathizer. This woman had a large growth in the upper part of her arm and was due to have an operation two days later to have it removed. The patient did not believe in Spiritual

Healing and was in a rather distraught condition. However, when the operation was performed, the growth had *diminished to approximately one-tenth of its size* and was not malignant.

CASE NUMBER 23.

A woman who had been suffering from severe pains in her back over a long period of time and who had been treated by doctors for many months, including a two-week stay in a hospital in traction, was given Contact Healing by a Member in the morning. She stated that as soon as the healer put their hands on her back, the severe pain left immediately. However, the next morning she was again in terrible pain and asked for a second Healing treatment. Again, when the healer's hands were put on her back, she stated the pain left immediately. After that she had no further trouble.

CASE NUMBER 24.

A woman friend of a Society Member learned from her doctor that she had multiple sclerosis. The Member placed her on the Absent Healing list and also gave her Contact Healing regularly. Since then, in the past year, the woman has experienced a fantastic change in her outlook on life. In a letter of appreciation, she says that she is now walking better and feeling happier. The depression which she was suffering from has also been lifted, she added.

CASE NUMBER 25.

After a Member of The Aetherius Society had appeared on television, she was contacted by a woman who had sustained a serious accident some twenty-three years before. She accompanied the Member on a Pilgrimage to Kinderscout the following Sunday and on the way showed her that she was unable to lift one leg. She had to wear a surgical corset with steel ribs after two unsuccessful bone grafts. Two days after the Pilgrimage she contacted the Member and excitedly said she could now lift the leg! The leg is now completely flexible.

CASE NUMBER 26.

A middle-aged woman sustained a hemorrhage and doctors suggested she would have to go into hospital and undergo an operation. As she was an active Staff Member of The Aetherius Society, she tried Spiritual Healing first, and after a couple of months the condition vanished and has never returned.

CASE NUMBER 27.

A woman with severe arthritis, who could virtually only hobble, came in for Healing. Afterwards, she threw away her stick and walked off unaided.

CASE NUMBER 28.

A senior healer at the London Headquarters of The Aetherius Society awoke one morning with a name in his mind recalled from a dream. A man came in for Healing later that day and stated that he had been "directed" to come in as someone could cure him of a slipped disc in his back. He saw the healer and said: "You're the one!" Although he had never done it before, the healer put the disc back in. On the way out he asked the man his name—and it was the same as the one in his dream!

CASE NUMBER 29.

Healing works, of course, particularly well on animals. A group of Aetherius Society Members on a Pilgrimage in the North of England, proved this to a gathering of climbers who were anxiously inspecting what looked to be a dead rabbit. They gave it Contact Healing to which it responded immediately, gradually regaining strength and finally hopping away. Said one climber: *"A miracle, a plain, straightforward miracle!"*

CASE NUMBER 30.

A kitten had been run over by a large heavy van and its back had apparently been broken. After Contact Healing, it completely recovered in a month.

CASE NUMBER 31.

A large young dog running in the park caught its foot in a hole and was howling with pain. The owner thought its foot was broken. Healing was given to the dog's foot and within five minutes it trotted off without even a limp—much to the owner's amazement and delight.

CASE NUMBER 32.

An apparently dead birch tree alongside its thriving fellows was given Contact Healing for ten minutes. Twenty-four hours later it had thrown out leaves in profusion just at the area where Healing was given. The rest of the leaves followed and weeks later it was as leafy as the others.

CASE NUMBER 33.

A patient had a heart attack on May 22, 1975, while driving his car. The rescue squad found him dead at the wheel and rushed him to the hospital. The patient had also injured his head in the ensuing accident. After heart massage, the patient was brought back to life but had brain damage, was unconscious, his head rolled back and forth, he did not recognize anyone, could not talk, swallow, or walk. The patient was put on the Absent Healing list on May 24 and within three or four days his head stopped rolling.

On June 25, two Members gave the patient Contact Healing in the hospital. He was instantly able to swallow food for the first time following treatment. He had talked a little previously, but it made no sense; he was now able to make sense when he spoke. About July 10, the patient was again given Contact Healing in hospital by two Members. He was then able to feed himself for the first time. In August, he could speak long sentences and raise his arms. After physical therapy, he was able to get on his feet. Both legs had been stiff: one in a straight position, one in a bent position. By September 22, he was at home, walking with a walker, talking normally, and an out-patient. His wife considers this a *"miracle,"* as the doctors had not expected him to live, and if he had, that he would have been incapable of coherent talk and would not even have been able to feed himself. Absent Healing is still being sent to this patient.

SUCCESS BY ABSENT HEALING

CASE NUMBER 34.

Absent Healing was sent for several weeks to a man suffering from haemophilia who had cut his foot. After this, the bleeding was considerably reduced and his condition improved.

CASE NUMBER 35.

An old woman suffering from incontinence was sent Absent Healing for several weeks and was completely cured.

CASE NUMBER 36.

A ten year old boy with leukemia was placed on the Absent Healing list. His head had become completely bald, but after twelve weeks he has shown a definite improvement. His hair is starting to grow again and he has no need to return to hospital.

CASE NUMBER 37.

A young girl, born with a rare disease (Glycogen Storage complaint) has been on the Absent Healing list for three years. She is still very small for her age, but is lively and intelligent. Doctors are amazed at her condition.

CASE NUMBER 38.

A Member of The Aetherius Society underwent a Mastectomy operation and was sent Healing by her colleagues before, during and afterwards. She said later that she felt a wonderful flow of Healing energy and that she felt more "whole" than at any time in her life.

CASE NUMBER 39.

A man with incurable cancer was suffering greatly. He had been given six months to live. After four Absent Healing services, he died *peacefully* in his sleep and his ordeal was brought to an end.

CASE NUMBER 40.

A young high-school girl was taken to hospital with glandular fever. It was later discovered she also had an illness called Hodgkins' Disease. She was in and out of hospital for two years as they tried every type of treatment: radium, Cobalt 60, iron medicine and operations to remove the spleen.

Naturally, the radiotherapy affected the system in retrograde ways as well and the glandular disease showed no signs of healing. One of the Officers of The Aetherius Society knew the girl well and held a special Healing service in London for her. Afterwards she also came to the Headquarters for treatment and has since received Absent Healing. Three years later, she is now working again and has gained in strength. *At one time, she was given only six months to live by a London consultant who studied her case and said it was hopeless.*

CASE NUMBER 41.

The mother of a Staff Member went into hospital for an emergency operation to remove an intestinal blockage. After three weeks, the blockage was removed by surgery and she was discharged. However, it appeared a couple of months later that the intestine was ulcerated where the blockage had occurred, resulting in a lot of pain and apparently requiring a further operation. But she had been placed on the Absent Healing lists of The Aetherius Society and when she returned to the hospital for a further examination, the doctors were amazed to discover that there was no trace of any ulceration. She was discharged again as completely fit and has remained in good health since then.

CASE NUMBER 42.

A young boy, age about eleven years, was suffering from Leukemia. His hair was falling out, he was very weak and could not eat. When placed on the Absent Healing list, he began to make a slight improvement. Four months later, he has made quite a recovery. He is now healthy, with a lovely head of curly hair, lively and living life as a boy of his age should. The doctors were amazed and could not account for the rapid improvement.

CASE NUMBER 43.

An elderly but active woman noticed that she had a growth on the side of her left breast, which later became hard and grew black in colour. She went to hospital to have ultra-violet treatment. The doctors could not define what the growth was but it was like a cancer growth. She could only receive this treatment about once a fortnight as this particular spot was tender and liable to burn, so therefore progress was slow. Then she was put on our Absent Healing list and the Member who had close contact with her also gave her Contact Healing. Within about two months, this black lump disappeared almost as quickly as it had appeared, which quite astounded the doctors, for they could not find any trace of it even after several X-rays.

CASE NUMBER 44.

A Member's husband was suffering from a bad foot which was causing him to limp. During the day the woman concentrated particularly hard on sending Healing power to her husband and later on he certified that at a particular time—when she was sending power to him—he felt energy was being sent to him. At that time—the pain just went and he did not have the limp any more.

CASE NUMBER 45.

A Member of The Aetherius Society suffered from quite severe food poisoning, which made her feel very ill and sick for the whole day. She had an important function the following day which she was afraid of missing. Other Members were contacted and Healing was sent to her. One Member also went to her home and gave Contact Healing. The following day she was able to get up and go out.

CASE NUMBER 46.

At the age of twelve years, the patient, a Thibetan refugee school boy, was taken into an Indian hospital suffering from tuberculosis of the spine. He underwent an operation in which seven vertebrae were fused together, without any support between each one. As the young boy grew the spine became less and less able to support it, until, semi-crippled as a young man of seventeen, the spine curved out under the left shoulder blade, distorting the whole thorax and restricting the lungs.

In 1972, he contracted tuberculosis again in the lungs and was put on the Society Absent Healing list. He slowly improved, but nearly died some months later when an air pocket in the lung accumulated enough stale air to cause pressure which collapsed the lung. He was advised that this could threaten his life at any time and he should always be within near distance to a hospital.

While his tuberculosis improved, his spinal condition deteriorated and doctors in India held out little hope for his survival, saying the only future was a collapse of the spine and paralysis. Expert doctors in England who examined his X-rays also advised that little could be done to help the young man and no one in such a state could survive long.

On top of this, the tuberculosis again broke out with a vengeance and was breaking through the barriers which the medicine builds up to contain it. It was on the point of flooding uncontrollably throughout the body. *He was given six months to live!*

That was over eighteen months ago. Now, while his spine is still not straight, it is definitely not worse, and has even strengthened. The tuberculosis has stopped spreading and, at this point in time, a first hand report from someone who has been with him throughout much of his illness, declares that he is looking better than he has for many years.

CASE NUMBER 47.

A man was given three months to live in October 1973, suffering from cancer of the lung which was inoperable. He was put on the Absent Healing list immediately, and a report at Christmas stated that the tumor had mysteriously stopped growing. Doctors could not understand why. He was operated on early in 1974 and a year later is still alive and doing very well.

CASE NUMBER 48.

A middle-aged woman, whose husband had just died, reacted in a very negative manner to this event. She withdrew into herself and became, in the words of the healer who eventually treated her: "A veritable living robot." She had no interest in herself, her family, or anything else. She used to talk to her husband all the time—even though he was no longer there. Since she was placed on the Absent Healing list, she has made a steady recovery and now leads a normal family life again.

CASE NUMBER 49.

A teenage girl was taken to hospital with an illness which affected her spine. The main symptom was that she was unable to bend from her waist and could not turn her head at all. The Doctors warned her that she could injure her spinal column severely if she did try to move and told her parents that she would have to miss school for between one and two years. Her name was put on the Absent Healing list and she started to improve immediately. Within four months she was released from hospital and has now completely recovered and is able to lead a normal life.

CASE NUMBER 50.

A patient had severe sugar diabetes since childhood and had taken insulin injections for at least thirty years. After being on the Absent Healing list for three and one-half years, she was cured and no longer had to take insulin injections. *The patient had not been told that Healing was sent to her!*

CASE NUMBER 51.

An active social worker requested Healing for intense pain, partial sensory paralysis, lethargy, depression and acute insomnia, which were the result of dental surgery a year earlier when four inches of a main nerve had been removed. A complicated system of Absent Healing was set up including Colour Healing and fluids impregnated with Spiritual energies. Immediately following the first treatment, the year's long insomnia was cured. Three days later, the paralysis and pain in the affected jaw had disappeared and after a week of treatment, most of the symptoms of her condition had disappeared. Within the next few weeks, she was completely cured and the cure has remained permanent *for the last ten years.....!*

CASE NUMBER 52.

Healing was requested for a child of four and a half years old suffering from chronic bronchitis, who had to be hospitalized for the third time in two years. He has not had any recurrence since; that was five years ago.

CASE NUMBER 53.

A middle-aged lady broke her leg, which was not set correctly and had to be broken again. After the break healed it was discovered that the knee joint no longer functioned properly and the doctor declared it was paralyzed. She was from then on only able to walk with two canes. Absent Healing was requested and after six months she was able to walk without canes, was entertaining again and was back to normal.

CASE NUMBER 54.

Absent Healing was requested for a patient just before he had major open heart surgery. He recovered within two weeks. **This was a case unheard of in history of medical science!** The chief cardiologist of Yale University examined him because it was such an outstanding Healing.

CASE NUMBER 55.

After a prostate gland operation, it was discovered that the X-rays also showed a damaged bladder and a doctor said an operation would be necessary. Absent Healing was requested and a month later the doctor re-examined the patient and found that the condition had completely healed. The doctor dismissed him, stating no operation was necessary at all.

CASE NUMBER 56.

An elderly lady had a slight stroke which left her vision impaired very severely and caused paralysis of the left hand and arm. She had moreover suffered from rheumatoid arthritis for many years. Absent Healing was requested and after only six sessions the left eye was completely normal again, all paralysis had disappeared. Definite improvement continued in the general health of the lady and two months later the right eye also was back to normal again.

CASE NUMBER 57.

A middle-aged lady had her husband write to say that she had come down with a severe crippling condition whereby she could not walk upright but had to crawl on hands and knees. Absent Healing was sent. After only a few sessions the lady was able to walk again with a cane and is well on the road to complete recovery from whatever it was that ailed her.

CASE NUMBER 58.

A stranger came to the door of the Church in the Los Angeles Headquarters of The Aetherius Society one morning, who had never been there before, saying that his wife, a young woman, had gone into a coma that morning for no apparent reason and was in hospital. Immediately thereafter, within five minutes of this visit, Absent Healing was sent.

A few hours later the man came back to say that his wife was well and was back home again. The doctors had been completely baffled by this case and had been unable to diagnose the illness.

CASE NUMBER 59.

A woman of seventy-two was suffering from cirrhosis of the liver and gallstones and it was not possible to operate on her. She went into a coma for three days and was put on the Absent Healing list. Within three months she had completely recovered and the gallstones had disappeared—much to the doctors' amazement.....!

CASE NUMBER 60.

A woman suffering from acute angina was put on the Absent Healing list. She recovered within a month and is still enjoying good health two years later.

CASE NUMBER 61.

A man whose pelvis was broken in several places was placed on the Absent Healing list. Within six months he was well and strong and able to walk normally.

CASE NUMBER 62.

A woman of ninety-five was very ill with Menieres Disease and also debility in general due to her great age. Within a month of being place on the Absent Healing list, she had recovered from her illness and is now amazingly fit for her age.

CASE NUMBER 63.

A woman suffering from gallstones was placed on the Absent Healing list and made a remarkable recovery very quickly. No operation was needed.

CASE NUMBER 64.

A young man was electrocuted on the overhead lines of a pylon and suffered third degree burns to his hands, arms and neck. He was taken to the intensive care unit of a hospital and also placed on the Absent Healing list. His burns have healed remarkably well.

CASE NUMBER 65.

A man in a serious motorcycle accident shattered his kneecap and left leg. After being put on the Absent Healing list, he recovered very well and a few months later was walking without the use of crutches.

CASE NUMBER 66.

A three-month old baby was in hospital with an unknown virus. He had excessive mucus in the lungs and stopped breathing twice. His condition was critical, but after being placed on the Absent Healing list, it improved rapidly and he was allowed home in four weeks. *The hospital were amazed, since this condition usually takes much longer to heal.*

CASE NUMBER 67.

A man who had contracted pneumonia in his youth had needed to use a breathing apparatus until he was given Absent Healing. A year later, he is still quite well again and does not need to use the apparatus.

CASE NUMBER 68.

The wife of a Branch Officer of The Aetherius Society suffered

from a duodenal ulcer from an early age. Her condition became so
bad that she had to go into hospital for an operation. Her name
was put on the Absent Healing list and after the operation her
condition improved so rapidly that she was released *within five
days!* In less than a month she had recovered enough to attend the
special Seminars which were held over four weekends.

CASE NUMBER 69.

A woman with violent abdominal pains was rushed into hospital for an operation. A Member of the Society who knew her well
learned of this and sent her Absent Healing after the operation, as
well as placing her on the Absent Healing list. The woman wrote to
her afterwards telling her that on the day she was sent Healing she
had had a strange experience in hospital. She was resting with her
eyes closed when she suddenly felt arms beneath her lifting her up.
She opened her eyes, fully expecting to find a nurse there, but there
was no one.

"I must stress that I was not asleep and it certainly was not a
dream," she says in her letter.

"My relatives, friends and neighbours consider that I have
made a remarkable recovery.....and I fully agree with them. I feel
that I must tell you about this and pray most sincerely that all
persons on your Absent Healing list receive the same benefit that I
have done."

CASE NUMBER 70.

A young boy who had been having fits was placed on the
Absent Healing list. He now has very few attacks and they do not
last as long as they did.

CASE NUMBER 71.

A car park attendant, crippled with arthritis from many years
work standing in water in a tannery, was sent Absent Healing by a
Member for several weeks. He is now better.

CASE NUMBER 72.

A man with a very serious heart condition was put on the Absent Healing list. He has made a good recovery and since then withstood influenza and a chest condition as well. He is being kept on the Absent Healing list.

CASE NUMBER 73.

A man with terminal cancer in Sweden was put on the Absent Healing list by the mother of a Member. Last Christmas he was allowed home to visit his family, although **doctors said he should have died by then.**

CASE NUMBER 74.

A colleague of a Member fell ill at work with suspected heart trouble. His pulse rate was very high and after tests and X-rays it was discovered by the hospital that he had an over-active thyroid gland. The specialist decided that once the pulse rate was brought under control, they would operate. The Member in question immediately placed the man's name on the Absent Healing list and within a month he was able to undergo the operation. The specialist told him they were amazed that his pulse rate had come down so quickly—it normally takes two or three months. After his operation he made a speedy recovery and is now working normally again.

CASE NUMBER 75.

A woman, who had been told she had terminal cancer by the hospital authorities in Jerusalem, returned to Britain, as she thought—to die. Her name was placed on the Absent Healing list and three months later the information was received that the woman had undergone a major operation and had come through successfully. *The doctors described it as a miraculous recovery* and the woman is now well enough to return to Jerusalem.

CASE NUMBER 76.

A woman with thrombosis following a bad fall downstairs, in which she put her knee through a window, was put on the Absent Healing list. Soon afterwards she made a complete recovery.

CASE NUMBER 77.

An operation was performed on a woman, aged thirty-two, who had a brain hemorrhage. She was put on the Absent Healing list when it was discovered she was ill and special Services were held for her. She was completely cured after three months and now lives a normal life.

CASE NUMBER 78.

After undergoing an operation for a cancerous growth, a patient was put on the Absent Healing list and made a remarkable recovery. After three months, as is the custom, her name was removed from the list. But she became ill again shortly afterwards and was operated on again for cancer. The same pattern happened twice more—after which her name was put on the list permanently, with strict instruction that it should not be removed. After a period of three years, during which she was under regular supervision by medical specialists and remained on the Healing list, she was pronounced completely cured by doctors, *who stressed that it was a "miraculous" event!*

CASE NUMBER 79.

A young man was found screaming with pain sitting in his car. He had noticed a fault with the car, stopped, lifted the bonnet and unscrewed the radiator cap. The steam, under pressure, had spouted straight into his eyes, over his face and scalded his hands. Several Aetherius Society Members gave him first aid, using homeopathic remedies, and then held a Healing Service for him in a secluded spot. Some twenty minutes later he was no longer in pain, despite the serious scalding he had received.

CASE NUMBER 80.

Two years ago, a Member in England was stricken with what is known as an incurable kidney complaint. She was taken to hospital and immediately Healing action was taken by Members throughout the Society. Although she technically "died" several times, a replacement kidney was found and she underwent a transplant. She survived this and with constant Healing has progressed remarkably well, so that several months ago she was able to make a Pilgrimage to Mount Madrigherfluh in Switzerland! (The full particulars of this case—a remarkable one—are described on page 14 of The Aetherius Society Newsletter, Volume 9, Issues 7, 8, 9 and 10, April & May 1970.)

AUTHOR'S NOTES:

Note 1. Application to either Headquarters of The Aetherius Society will bring free literature regarding the Holy Rocks from Charged Mountains which are mounted in handmade wooden Shapes which contain Mystical powers.

Note 2. For further information regarding the numerous activities of The Aetherius Society read "The Age Of Aetherius" written by Kevin Quinn Avery and Doctor George King and obtainable from the publishers, The Aetherius Society.

Note 3. The book "Contact Your Higher Self Through Yoga" written by Doctor George King is obtainable from the publishers, The Aetherius Society.

CHAPTER TEN

CONCLUSION

The list of successes goes on, case after case of remarkable results brought about by the use of my perfectly balanced Healing technique. To repeat, the true reports in the last Chapter are but a cross section taken from the scores of amazing results in Spiritual Healing brought about by a group of dedicated Members of The Aetherius Society in Los Angeles, Detroit and the European Headquarters. This brief cross section of case histories should give all readers of this book faith in the technique and in your own abilities when you consider that the results you have just read were brought about by ordinary, Spiritually-minded people, who diligently applied the techniques described in this book which I have taught them through the years.

Not even mentioned in the published case histories were the scores of Healings brought about during public meetings in London and other cities when a large band of our Spiritual healers gave repeated demonstrations of the effectiveness of this technique from the public platforms. At these meetings, people from the audience were invited to come up to the platform and have Spiritual Healing. They did so, many of them reporting immediate relief from the treatments.

The dozens of people who constitute the Healing bands of our organization know from first hand experience that this technique is one of the most powerful Spiritual Healing techniques ever developed. They will readily give testimony to this, as indeed will the hundreds of patients who have received so much benefit from the application of this technique throughout the years.

There are very few things that the ordinary, decent-minded man can do for others which will give him a deeper inner satisfaction than to help less fortunate people through their suffering and disease. Indeed, when you start Spiritual Healing seriously, you will find a whole new world of Service is opened up to you; a world in which you, with the right motive and knowledge, can function to help your less fortunate fellow men. As well as helping the sufferer, you will also help your own progression and the still, small, Divine voice of conscience within you will tell you that this is true.

You will also discover that many of your own troubles will be transmuted in the act of unselfish Service to others, because you can now help to Heal them. We all know that in this sick and suffering world, there is so much Spiritual Healing to be done.

May God protect and guide you all.